THE CURIOUS INCIDENT OF THE DOG IN THE NIGHT-TIME

Mark Haddon

AUTHORED by Zara Walters
UPDATED AND REVISED by Elizabeth Weinbloom

COVER DESIGN by Table XI Partners LLC
COVER PHOTO by Olivia Verma and © 2005 GradeSaver, LLC

BOOK DESIGN by Table XI Partners LLC

Published by GradeSaver LLC, www.gradesaver.com

First published in the United States of America by GradeSaver LLC. 2011

GRADESAVER, the GradeSaver logo and the phrase "Getting you the grade since 1999" are registered trademarks of GradeSaver, LLC

ISBN 978-1-60259-255-1

Printed in the United States of America

For other products and additional information please visit
http://www.gradesaver.com

Table of Contents

Table of Contents

Biography of Haddon, Mark (1962-)

The son of an architect, Mark Haddon was born in Northampton, England in 1962 and studied English at Merton College, Oxford. He became a carer for disabled people in Scotland after university, an experience which would inform his later work. His first writing work was as a children's author and illustrator.

Haddon is most famous for his novel *The Curious Incident of the Dog in the Night-time* which won the Whitbread Book of the Year Award in 2003 and the Commonwealth Writers' Prize Overall Best First Book in 2004. This novel was the first Haddon wrote specifically for an adult audience, although it was eventually marketed to both adults and children. Haddon's earlier works include the children's series *Agent Z*. He also wrote the screenplay adaptation of Raymond Brigg's story *Fungus the Bogeyman* which was screened on BBC1 in 2004. In 2009 Haddon donated his short story *The Island* to Oxfam's 'Ox-Tales' project.

Haddon is a vegetarian as well as a hard line atheist who lives in Oxford with his wife, Dr. Sos Eltis, a Fellow of Brasenose College, and their two sons. He enjoys canoeing, cycling and running marathons.

About The Curious Incident of the Dog in the Night-time

Published in 2003, *The Curious Incident of the Dog in the Night-time* has won more than 17 literary awards, including the Whitbread Book of the Year Award, sold more than 10 million copies and grossed £14 million in 2004 alone.

Haddon admits that he began the novel wanting to find a 'gripping and vivid' image that would stick in the reader's head. It was only once he had thought of the image of the dog with a fork sticking out of it that the voice of the narrator came to him. Haddon explains that 'only after a few pages did I really start to ask, *Who does the voice belong to?* So Christopher came along, in fact, after the book had already got underway.' He describes how he cracked the puzzle of the novel by explaining that 'if Christopher were real he would find it very hard, if not impossible, to write a book. The one thing he cannot do is put himself in someone else's shoes, and the one thing you have to do if you write a book is put yourself in someone else's shoes. The reader's shoes...The answer I came up with is having him be a fan of Sherlock Holmes stories. That way, he doesn't have to put himself in the mind of a reader. He just has to say, I enjoy Sherlock Holmes stories and I'll try to do something similar to that.'

Haddon believes the book he had most in mind when he was writing *The Curious Incident of the Dog in the Night-time* was Jane Austen's *Pride and Prejudice*. In a note about the novel, Haddon explains that Jane Austen was writing about boring people with limited lives and that were she alive today, she would be writing about chartered accountants in Welwyn Garden city. In *Pride and Prejudice* she writes about their lives with such empathy that they seem interesting, in the kind of book that her characters would read - the romantic novel. In *The Curious Incident of the Dog in the Night-time* that is what Haddon says he was trying to do: 'to take a life that seemed horribly constrained, to write about it in the kind of book that the hero would read - a murder mystery - and hopefully show that if you viewed this life with sufficient imagination it would seem infinite.'

Haddon explains that writing about disability thows light on things that might otherwise seem ordinary: 'It isn't entirely comfortable' he explains, but it show us 'how little separates us from those we turn away from in the street. It's about how badly we communicate with one another.'

Character List

Christopher John Francis Boone

At the start of the novel, Christopher is 15 years, 3 months and 2 days old. Christopher has Asperger's syndrome and is the narrator of this novel. He has the difficult relationship with other people common to those with severe Asperger's, and he doesn't like to be touched. He is incapable of telling lies. When he finds out about Wellington's death, he decides to begin a search for his killer. He is ambitious and wants to be a scientist. He is interested in the stars and science and the universe and by the end of the novel manages to take his A-level in maths.

Wellington

Mrs Shears' poodle. Wellington is found dead by Christopher at the very beginning of the novel, with a garden fork sticking out of him. The discovery prompts Christopher to begin 'detecting' to find out who killed him. This is the catalyst for the whole novel.

Ed Boone

Christopher's father. He works in the boiler business. He is the sole caregiver of Christopher, and has been since Christopher's mother died, two years before the start of the novel. Christopher's father looks after Christopher, knows all his habits, and understands the way Christopher works, but when he finds out that his son is trying to solve who killed Mrs. Shears' dog he becomes unusually angry and impatient. We learn that he killed the dog and that he lied about Christopher's mother being dead, and this prompts Christopher to leave home and make his first journey alone.

Siobhan

Christopher's friend of eight years and a member of the staff at his school, where he studies with other children with learning difficulties. To help Christopher understand human emotion, she draws faces for him so that he can identify that a smile means happy, a frown means angry and so on. It is Siobhan who sets the assignment that propels Christopher to write his novel, and she gives him writing tips throughout. She is very patient with Christopher and encourages his writing.

Mrs. Eileen Shears

Owner of Wellington, the poodle. A neighbor and friend of Ed's, she lives on the opposite side of the road, two houses to the left. She screams and screams when she sees Christopher with her dead dog. When she sees the dog spouting blood from the holes that have pierced it with the fork she doesn't pick it up. Christopher thinks this might be because she doesn't want to get dirty. These clues might lead to understanding her character but because Christopher doesn't deal with 'character' in a standard way, it is difficult to tell. We learn later in the novel that

Mrs Shears' husband ran off with Christopher's mother, Judy. Later, Mrs. Shears had a relationship with Ed Boone. The relationship turned sour, which is what prompted Ed to attack the dog.

Mrs. Alexander

Another (older) lady who lives on Christopher's street, at number 39. Mrs. Alexander offers Christopher squash and biscuits when he visits her. Even when his father forbids him from interviewing the neighbors about Wellington, Christopher speaks to her. He asks her if Mr. Shears may have wanted to upset Mrs. Shears, and she reveals that Mr. Shears and Christopher's mother had an affair before she died.

Judy Boone

Christopher's mother. We are told very early on that Christopher's mother died two years ago - there was something wrong with her heart, and Christopher didn't visit her at the hospital. When Christopher discovers letters from his mother in his father's room, he realizes that his father was lying. He no longer trusts his father. He begins his journey to London to find his mother, who is living with Mr. Shears. She finds Christopher hard work, and when Christopher and Mr. Shears do not get along, she says she is only just managing to keep it together. At the end of the novel, Judy has moved back to Swindon and Christopher is living with her.

Toby

Christopher's pet rat. Christopher looks after him and feeds him and cares for him very well. Christopher rescues Toby from the tracks of the London Underground by jumping off the platform and searching for him, and manages to get out just before a train comes. Toby is the companion that Christopher takes with him on his journey to find his mother.

Mr. Roger Shears

Used to be married to Mrs. Shears until he ran off with Christopher's mother to London. He is the initial suspect in Christopher 'detecting'. When Christopher arrives at his house, having been searching for Judy, Roger is cruel to him and says 'You think you're so fucking clever, don't you? Don't you ever think about other people?' He totally misunderstands Christopher, and so Judy leaves him and moves back to Swindon with her son.

Uncle Terry

Christopher's uncle who lives in Sunderland and works in a bread factory.

Grandma Burton

Christopher's grandmother who lives in a home and has senile dementia.

Terry

A boy at school - older brother of Francis - tells Christopher that he will 'only ever get a job collecting supermarket trollies or cleaning out donkey shit at an animal sanctuary' and that 'they didn't let spazzers drive rockets that cost billions of pounds.' Having told us what Terry says, Christopher writes that he is going to go to University and study maths and/or physics.

Mrs. Peters

Teaches art at school and helps Christopher make a Get Well Soon card for his mother, when she is in hospital.

Mrs Gascoyne

Headmistress of Christopher's school. She doesn't want him to take A level Maths because she says the school doesn't have the facilities for students to sit A-levels, but when Ed shouts at her she concedes.

Reverend Peters

Mrs. Peters' husband, who comes into school to talk about God and heaven. He can't answer Christopher's questions about where heaven is or where God is.

Rhodri

A friend of Ed's who also works in maintenance and who occasionally joins Ed for a drink while they watch TV.

Major Themes

The written word

Everything in *The Curious Incident of the Dog in the Night-Time* is seen through the eyes of Christopher, the fifteen-year-old genius narrator with Asperger's syndrome. All events are processed through his remarkable mind. Very early on we are made aware that the novel Christopher starts writing is the novel we have in our hands. For that reason we always feel close to Christopher: we are not only looking out on the world from his perspective but we are literally positioned in his shoes, holding the very novel that he is holding as he writes. We are effectively written into his story. For this reason we become more and more tuned into the way in which Christopher views the world. The emotional outbursts of those around Christopher are told in a matter-of-fact way that makes episodes of rage somehow distant and often even more chilling. We are let into his world in a way that other characters in the novel seem not to have access. Haddon endows us with the necessary equipment (this novel) to be able to understand Christopher and to share his life and as a result we are introduced into the world of this young man in a way that no other character in the novel can fully do. It is a gift that Haddon has given us and it is a testament to the power of writing and communicating.

The way in which Christopher uncovers perhaps the greatest secret of the novel is no accident – there is a reason why he finds out that his mother is alive by reading letters from her. Christopher uncovers the truth by reading. Through reading his mother's letters he is able to digest the information in his own way and in his own time. This is exactly what Haddon gifts us with: Christopher's narrative is so simple and yet uncovers a world of complex truths. His logic and matter-of-fact attitude allow us to see the world fresh. The unique perspective of Christopher's logic colors everything in the narrative. Mark Haddon is writing a story about Christopher writing a story, and Christopher is writing a story that forces us to re-write our own stories.

God, order and stability

Christopher tells us in Chapter 199 that 'people believe in God because the world is very complicated and they think it is very unlikely that anything as complicated as a flying squirrel or the human eye or a brain could happen by chance. But they should think logically and if they thought logically they would see that they can only ask this question because it has already happened and they exist.'

Christopher's sense of stability and order comes from understanding science and logic - he does not feel comforted by holding on to the idea that there is a greater power controlling what we do and what will happen. In Christopher's world, if there were a greater power controlling things then he would not have the free will that he is confident he has. This endows Christopher, and each character, with their own individuality.

Christopher's sense of order is constructed by himself and not dictated to him. For instance when Christopher sees lots of red cars in a row, he knows it is going to be a good day. He explains in Chapter 47 that 'Mr Jeavons, the psychologist at the school, once asked me why 4 red cars in a row made it a **Good Day**, and 3 red cars in a row made it a **Quite Good Day**, and 5 red cars in a row made it a **Super Good Day** and why 4 yellow cars in a row made it a **Black Day**, which is a day when I don't speak to anyone and sit on my own reading books and don't eat my lunch...I said that I liked things to be in a nice order...And I said that some people who worked in an office came out of their house in the morning and saw that the sun was shining and it made them feel happy, or they saw that it was raining and it made them feel sad [but]...in an office the weather didn't have anything to do with whether they had a good day or a bad day.'

Christopher acknowledges that he needs order in his life and acknowledges that the order we each chose for ourselves is comforting but not logical.

Autism, language and communication

Although the word is not mentioned in the novel, Christopher does suffer from Asperger's syndrome, which is an autistic spectrum disorder. This means that Christopher expresses himself in a simple and straightforward way and cannot understand commonly accepted modes of signaling. For instance, he says 'I find people confusing. This is for two main reasons. The first main reason is that people do a lot of talking without using any words...The second main reason is that people often talk using metaphors.' Christopher does not accept the typical 'signals' that people use to communicate, for instance 'raising an eyebrow' which Siobhan explains to him 'can mean 'I want to do sex with you' and it can also mean 'I think that what you just said was very stupid.'

The fact that Christopher has a form of autism allows Haddon to take away the baggage that language has adopted over the years and to strip it bare once again to a pure form; we have to interact directly with the words that are spoken and not with the implications of these words according to the society we live in. In this way, Christopher's account allows us to see the world in a new and fresh light without taking anything for granted. He says himself 'My name...means *carrying Christ*...Mother used to say that it meant Christopher was a nice name because it was a story about being kind and helpful, but I do not want my name to mean a story about being kind and helpful. I want my name to mean me.' Christopher's father fans out his fingers and touches Christopher 'and it means that he loves me' .

Christopher does not like to be hugged. He does not understand what different facial expressions are. He needs to relate directly and individually to language; through his writing, language is reborn in less encumbered way. Most of us would understand what 'I laughed my socks off' meant but few of us would know where the expression originated, and so we have lost the impact of the metaphor because we don't know why it is used in this way. Christopher forces us to reassess our relationship with language so that it speaks directly to us and so that the only tool we use to communicate is a direct reflection of what we think and feel, not a borrowed or inherited means of expression.

Detective story

The novel is set up as a detective story from the outset. Christopher wants to work out who killed Mrs. Shears' dog, Wellington. He sets out to find out about *The Curious Incident of the Dog in the Night-time* but instead finds out much more about his own life and family. The title represents what Christopher hopes to find out but within the title itself is another world of mystery that is uncovered as we go through the novel.

This detective novel is multi-layered. Christopher believes he is in control of his narrative and of the investigation because he believes he is an outsider who will go 'inside' this story, investigate, and find out the truth. In actual fact, as Christopher starts to write and to find out more information, the narrative runs away with itself and it is no longer Christopher who is in control. As he documents his findings, we realize that in actual fact Christopher is not an outside to this investigation at all: the mystery lies in his own house. Christopher calls his novel a 'murder mystery novel' but he will not have known how poignant a description that is. Wellington's murderer is of course Ed, his father, but Ed could also be accused of another murder: that of his mother. Although not really dead, Ed murdered Christopher's mother when he lied and told his son that she had died. When we realize this, Ed's explanation that she had 'a problem with her heart' becomes all the more unsettling.

This is not the only 'detecting' that goes on in the novel. At the outset, Christopher's view of the world and his reaction to it may seem unusual. However, Christopher's consistent logic and mathematical reason educate the reader, and as we read the novel we go on a journey and learn more and more about Christopher. By the end we empathize more with Christopher than we do with his parents, or Mr. Shears. We understand his impulses and there is security in his inability to tell a lie. As we have followed him on this journey of investigation, we have uncovered much more than just who killed Wellington: we have learned all about a very gifted boy who has Asperger's syndrome. This surely must alter what we usually take for granted about our own perspective on life.

Tragedy

It is interesting to think of this novel in terms of a 'tragedy'. After all, in his search for truth, Christopher uncovers a mystery that not only implicates him and his family but also causes a major shift in his family: he moves out and lives with his mother.

The structure of the novel could be compared to that of a tragedy. but it does not end in misery. By the end of the novel, Christopher has made the journey to the other side and essentially brought his mother back from the dead. It is almost as though Christopher, by adhering strictly to his own criteria of behavior, has escaped the trap of literature and has escaped the tragedy. As Polonius says in *Hamlet*, 'to thine own self be true/And it must follow, as the night the day/Thou canst not then be false to any man.' Unlike Hamlet, Macbeth, Lear or Othello, Christopher lives his life by his own standards, is not poisoned by what other people think, does not shy away from what he thinks is right, does not try to get ahead by being unfair and does not regard his own status at all. It is perhaps for this reason that despite the horrifying information he uncovers about his family, he is able to rise out of the misery and redeem all of the characters in the novel.

Science and Art

Christopher writes the novel because he wants to record his experience of 'detecting'. He adheres to his own rules about structure and form and only occasionally nods to more typical ways of writing – for instance when Siobhan tells him to include more description in his writing. When he decides to include more description, he does so in a way that interests him, for instance when he describes the sky. Christopher breaks the mold and instinctively expresses what comes to him as he writes. Haddon of course has constructed a very tight narrative in order for it to feel as instinctive and fresh as it does.

Haddon's mathematical structure in *The Curious Incident of the Dog in the Night-time* is carefully constructed. Haddon knew that in order to be able to communicate the thoughts of a boy like Christopher he must find a realistic reason for him to write a book. And so Christopher is made to love detective novels. Haddon sets up an almost scientific set of circumstances in order to enable him to create this work of art.

This is mirrored throughout the novel – Christopher wants to be a scientist and is actually a novelist. Christopher believes in logic and in science and interestingly it is his imagination that takes him on this 'detecting' journey that enables him to uncover more than he could ever have thought possible. He would never have imagined the twist that takes place, and yet it is his imagination as he is searching for Wellington's killer that brings him to the realization. Of course it is Haddon's imagination that constructs such a mathematically brilliant structure, which means that when we discover that Christopher's mother is indeed alive, it is a huge shock.

Love and relationships

Christopher's inability to express his feelings of love and closeness in a typical manner can feel alienating. If you did not understand Christopher you might not believe he was capable of feelings of love in the way in which most people understand. However, Christopher once again teaches us the importance of reassessing our own definitions. Even though he does not like to be hugged by his father and even though he shows no obvious signs of missing his mother, Haddon manages to construct a world in which we are genuinely touched by Christopher's honesty about his feelings. Remembering his mother, he explains that she smelt nice which is such a specific memory that it conjures up a whole image of Christopher being physically close to his mother and feeling comforted by her familiar smell.

The big mistake that Christopher's father makes is to hide the information from Christopher that his mother is leaving them because he wants to 'protect' his son. Presumably worrying that Christopher will feel rejected, he hides this vital information from him. Christopher's response to this, however, is not as one might expect - when he eventually finds his mother he is not angry that she left him. His relationships are conducted differently than ours.

Christopher shows that he is more caring that most people who express their love in the usual ways. When he notices that Toby is missing, he puts his own life in danger in order to save him.

Once again, Christopher makes us reassess how we view relationships. Since the traditional marital relationships of the novel are not very successful, it is clear that the way in which the rest of us deal with love and relationships is not necessarily ideal.

Glossary of Terms

Amnesia
Loss of memory

Apocryphal
Of questionable authorship or authenticity.

Battenberg cake
A sponge cake with a pink-and-yellow checkered pattern.

Dachshund dog
A small dog with short legs and a long body.

Ecosystem
A biological system composed of all the organisms found in a particular physical environment, interacting with it and with each other.

Giddy
Dizzy, overwhelmed, prone to vertigo.

Hypotenuse
In a right triangle, the side opposite the right angle.

Hypothetical
Conjectural, supposed or assumed.

Luminous
Full of light; emitting or casting light; shining, bright.

Marks and Spencer
A British chain of department stores, specializing in clothing and luxury food.

Metaphor
A comparison that does not use "like" or "as."

Pellet
A small, round substance.

Pythagoras' theorem

A basic theorem of Euclidean geometry, describing the relationship between the sides of any right triangle. The sum of the square of the two sides that make up the right angle, the theorem says, will equal the square of the remaining side.

Resonant frequencies

Some particles will oscillate more widely at some frequencies than at others - such a frequency is said to be the resonant frequency.

Rhetorical question

A figure of speech in which a question is posed for effect, rather than in expectation of a reply.

Schizophrenic

A mental disorder often characterized by vivid hallucinations.

Silhouette

The tracing of a person's shadow to create a portrait.

Simile

A comparison using 'like' or 'as'.

Stanley knife

A cutting tool used for a variety of purposes.

Swiss Army Knife

A multi-tool pocket knife.

Short Summary

Christopher Boon, a mathematically gifted boy of fifteen with Asperger's syndrome, sees a dog lying on the grass in front of his neighbor's house with a fork sticking out of it. The dog is dead. He goes over to hug the dog and soon the neighbor, Mrs Shears, emerges from her house, screaming. She thinks Christopher has killed the dog.

The police arrive and Christopher is taken to the station and, shortly after, his father arrives to testify for Christopher and take him home. The strange death of Wellington prompts Christopher to search for his killer. As a school assignment, Christopher's class is told to write a story. Inspired by this, he decides to write a detective story, the very one we are reading: The Curious Incident of the Dog in the Night-time.

Taking his inspiration from the *Sherlock Holmes* stories, Christopher knocks on the doors of various neighbors to try to find out what happened to Wellington. His father is furious when he finds out what Christopher is doing, and forbids him from continuing his 'detecting'. Not understanding the logic behind his father's aggression or his insistence that he stop, Christopher continues his search and talks to one of his neighbors, Mrs Alexander. Christopher asks her about Mrs Shears and asks, since Mr Shears left his wife, if she thought he had something to do with the murder. Mrs Alexander reveals that Mrs Shears and Christopher's mother were having an affair, before Christopher's mother died two years before.

Not long after, Christopher's father discovers his book, screams at Christopher, grabs him and throws his book away. While at work, Christopher looks for his book among his father's belongings and finds letters addressed to him, from his mother at an address in London, written a year and a half after she died. Once Christopher realizes his father lied to him, he feels sick and lies in bed. His father finds him and realizes what has happened and apologizes, telling Christopher he was only trying to protect him and that he can trust him. He then tells Christopher that it was he who killed Wellington because, after a relationship with Mrs Shears when Christopher's mother had left, he had an argument with her and the dog came after him and all his feelings just came bubbling up.

Terrified by the news of his father as a murderer, Christopher slips out of the house with his pet rat Toby and a swiss army knife while his father is asleep. He starts his journey to find his mother in London. The police have been informed that Christopher is running away and they try to catch him. At one point during the journey he loses Toby and follows him along the tube tracks, getting back onto the platform just before the train arrives.

Christopher finally arrives at his mother's and tells her what has happened and that he thought she was dead. He goes to sleep and wakes up to hear his father shouting.

His father enters Christopher's room and tries to apologize. Christopher won't talk to his father and insists he lives with his mother, thus ending her relationship with Mr Shears. He takes his A-level in maths and finally allows his father back into his life. His father suggests that they work on a project together where he proves to Christopher that he can be trusted and, to show how serious he is, buys a puppy that they can look after together. They begin spending more time together. Christopher plans to take further maths A-level a year later, and then physics A-level, and then he plans to get a first class honors degree and become a scientist – he knows this is possible because he solved a mystery, went to London alone and wrote a book.

Quotes and Analysis

It sounds like white noise everywhere, which is like silence but not empty.

p.130, Christopher

Christopher likes white noise because it blocks out the sound of other things happening in the world. It allows him to concentrate. The noise is peaceful. Having some sound allows him to feel connected to the world, because he knows that by hearing the sound, he exists in the world.

Prime numbers is what is left when you have taken all the patterns away

Christopher, p.15

Christopher says in Chapter 29 that his name means *carrying Christ* and he says 'I do not want my name to mean a story about being kind and helpful. I want my name to mean me.'

Equally, Christopher chooses to give his chapters prime numbers because he likes them: they mean something to him. He does not choose prime numbers because they have significance for someone else, like his name meaning carrying Christ. Also like him, prime numbers do not fit in with a typical or easy pattern - they are difficult to identify and they are a rule unto no one.

His face was drawn but the curtains were real.

Ed's joke, as told by Christopher p. 10

This is a joke made by Christopher's father that Christopher repeats to us. Using this example as a blueprint for jokes, Christopher tells us that there won't be any jokes in his novel, at least of this sort. This joke is exactly the sort of slippery sentence that Christopher finds difficult to fathom. Although he understands that the joke works because of the three different meanings of drawn, he does not understand the logic of it, and of course the point is that there is no logic to it: why would a direct comparison be made between a face and curtains? What is exposed here is not that Christopher is incapable of thinking like us and understanding a joke, but rather that he sees through the transparency of the joke and realizes that the pun does not make up for the fact that the sentence itself is essentially nonsense.

Mother was a small person who smelt nice

'My memory has a smelltrack which is like a soundtrack'. This is what Christopher says later on in the novel. It is significant therefore that, to him, his mother smelt 'nice'. Although Christopher thinks his mother is dead, he does not show much emotion about it. When Christopher recollects the day he found out his mother had died, he never describes how he felt - he is simply very practical about what might have caused her heart attack and what sort of a heart attack it was. It is quite significant therefore that his description of her includes his own personal appreciation of her smell, making this description quite moving.

This is another reason why I don't like proper novels, because they are lies about things which didn't happen and they make me feel shaky and scared.

And this is why everything I have written here is true.

Christopher says that he cannot tell lies because 'there is only ever one thing which happened at a particular time and a particular place. And there are an infinite number of things which didn't happen at that time and that place. And if I think about something which didn't happen I start thinking about all the other things which didn't happen.'

Christopher's imagination can't cope with the scope of possibilities in life. He must only relate what he knows to be factually true, putting his readers in a very secure position: we know that we will be given the truth as far as he knows. Any factually incorrect information in the manuscript is Christopher's error, not Christopher's willful misleading.

People believe in God because the world is very complicated and they think it is very unlikely that anything as complicated as a flying squirrel or the human eye or a brain could happen by chance. But they should think logically and if they thought logically they would see that they can only ask this question because it has already happened and they exist. And there are billions of planets where there is no life, but there is no one on those planets with brains to notice.

Christopher's clear-sightedness here is quite brutal and can be seen as an example of his relative insensitivity to other the way other people view the world. At the same time, his argument here is also a very sensible one and one that is difficult to argue with - we see therefore how his logical relationship with the world can be at once alienating as well as crystal clear.

I was excited. When I started writing my book there was only one mystery to solve. Now there were two.

Christopher, p. 124

This is Christopher's response when he first discovers a letter which appeared to have been written by his mother and sent from London. Thinking that his mother is dead and not believing that she has ever lived in London, this is a very confusing find for Christopher. He even considers that the letter is meant for a different Christopher. He is excited by the challenge of finding out why and when this letter had been written and not at all impatient to find out whether it was his mother. He decides to wait until the next time his father is out of the house to find out. This is another example of Christopher's unique reaction to the letter. He will become emotionally involved when he discovers what it means, but first of all it is a practical problem that needs solving.

My memory is like a film. That is why I am really good at remembering things, like the conversations I have written down in this book, and what people were wearing, and what they smelled like, because my memory has a smelltrack which is like a soundtrack.

Christopher, p. 96

This is a key characteristic of Christopher's thinking: the images and scenes he narrates for us have such clarity that we are swept up into his world and are really able to access his viewpoint. We are also able to view the other characters with a renewed clarity, and so the novel really does educate the reader, not only about Christopher and his perspective but about altogether seeing the world from a fresh angle.

And I would be able to look out of a little window in the spacecraft and know that there was no one else near me for thousands and thousands of miles which is what I sometimes pretend at night in the summer when I go and lie on the lawn and look up at the sky and I put my hands round the sides of my face so that I can't see the fence and the chimney and the washing line and I can pretend I'm in space.

Christopher, p. 66

This is Christopher's spiritual existence - seeing himself in relation to the universe. He says that he wants to be an astronaut, and his respect and admiration for the universe is clearly deep seated. This is his escape from the world as we know it, full of man-made commodities. We know that he does not accept the way everyone else sees the world, and this is his connection with something he utterly admires and feel connected to: a logical mathematical world that functions because of the detailed precision of its genius.

And then I thought that I had to be like Sherlock Holmes and had to detach my mind at will to a remarkable degree so that I did not notice how much it was hurting inside my head.

Christopher, p. 164

Equating himself here to another astutely logical thinker, Sherlock Holmes, Christopher is able to disconnect himself from the world and enter his own mental space. Like Holmes, he disconnects in order to think clearly and without distraction. Unlike Holmes (as written by Doyle, at any rate), Christopher also acknowledges that the emotional distance is a protection from hurt.

Quotes and Analysis

Summary and Analysis of Section 1

Chapter 2

The narrator describes how, at seven minutes after midnight, he sees a dog 'lying on the grass in the middle of the lawn in front of Mrs Shears' house.' He sees that it is lying on its side, and that it has a garden fork sticking out of it. He wonders who could have killed it.

Chapter 3

The narrator introduces himself as Christopher John Francis Boone. He says he knows 'all the countries in the world and their capital cities and every prime number up to 7507.' He describes how, when he met Siobhan eight years ago, she showed him a picture of a sad face. He describes how he understood the picture to mean sad and so told her to draw several faces so that when people spoke to him and he couldn't detect their mood, he could refer to his drawings for help. Siobhan laughs at him, and draws a picture of a puzzled face, telling him that he would make people feel weird if he did that. So he stops and says that if he doesn't know how to read people's moods in the future, he will simply ask them or walk away.

Chapter 5

Christopher tells how he pulls the fork out of the dog who was leaking blood from the fork holes. He hugs the dog and appreciates how straight-forward dogs are: 'You always know what a dog is thinking. It has four moods. Happy, sad, cross and concentrating.' Four minutes later, Mrs Shears runs towards Christopher and shouts 'What in fuck's name have you done to my dog?' Christopher narrates that he does not like people shouting at him because it makes him scared and because he worries that they are going to hit or touch him. He puts his hands over his ears and hunches into a ball on the cold wet grass.

Chapter 7

This section begins: 'This is a murder mystery novel.' Christopher explains that Siobhan told him he should write something that he would want to read. She suggested that he starts the novel with something that grabs people's attention. That is why he starts with the dog, he explains. He says he also started with the dog because it was an incident that happened to him - he finds things that don't happen to him hard to imagine. Siobhan says he should write about a person and not a dog but Christopher says that he wanted to write about something real and that dogs were 'faithful and honest'.

Analysis

It is very interesting that from the outset Christopher is interested in understanding peoples' moods, and that the novel starts by him feeling comfortable with understanding a dog's mood. Beginning with a dead dog tells us something about Christopher's loneliness and inability to communicate with the outside world.

The novel is set up as a detective from the outset – a simple who-done-it. What it sets up is a premise for exploration and for investigation; for Christopher, it is an opportunity to find a concrete and definite answer to the mystery. It is mathematical in its structure and yet, as we are to learn, the puzzle is not as black and white as Christopher expects.

What the novel sets up is almost a child-like situation. Christopher sees this dog with holes in it – the way he describes it makes it seem much less than it is. It is described is as though we are looking at a comic book, so from the start the reader is distanced by the tone of the writing. We are viewing the world through unfamiliar eyes.

We are not sure when we read 'This is a murder mystery novel' if the sentence refers to the book we are reading or to the book that Christopher goes on to say he has been encouraged to write by Siobhan. We soon realize that they are one and the same and that this section states how he ended up writing the novel, which he is only 5 pages into writing!

Christopher footnotes the following quote: 'I am veined with iron, with silver and with streaks of common mud. I cannot contract into the firm fist which those clench who do not depend on stimulus.' He uses this quote to explain that he does not generally like 'proper novels' because they contain sentences, like this one, that he does not understand. It is a quote from Virginia Woolf's *The Waves*. The quote seems to suggest that the person 'veined with iron, with silver and with streaks of common mud' has the potential to be decisive and strong (iron, silver) but is also base and cowardly (mud) which perhaps stops them from being able to act decisively and without doubt, which closely associates itself with *Hamlet*. It is therefore significant that this sentence is incomprehensible to Christopher (and note, also to his family).

The description of Siobhan is entirely physical: she 'has long blonde hair and wears glasses which are made of green plastic.' Christopher is very straight-forward and sees unusually. It is as though he sees each thing as if for the first time - as though he reassesses afresh each time he experiences something. It is like reading a book and reading the words, without reading subtext or creating atmosphere or imagining scenes. As he says of his book; 'it is a puzzle.' He decides to write about a dog because he doesn't have access to the subtleties and complexities of human emotion (as seen in 3 with the diagrams) and so he trust dogs because they are clear and honest.

Due to the narrator's authorial voice being very present in the text, Mark Haddon becomes Christopher John Francis Boone. We are drawn into the art of writing and so the dichotomy between maths and art is set up: what does it take to write a novel?

A mathematical and logical sense of structure and an understanding of people's feelings. Yet Christopher claims he cannot fathom people's feelings. But he is so in touch with his own that it is all that we, as readers, need.

Summary and Analysis of Section 2

Chapter 11

He goes back into the story: two policemen arrive - one man and one woman. The policeman asks Christopher what he was doing. The policeman then asks why Christopher was holding the dog and he does not know how to respond. Because he likes holding it, he thinks to himself. The policeman keeps asking questions, asking him if he killed the dog and Christopher narrates that he is asking too many questions and asking them too quickly. He compares his mind to a bread factory where his Uncle Terry works - 'the slicer is not working fast enough but the bread keeps coming and there is a blockage.' Christopher moans on the grass to block the noise (as he does with the radio, tuning it between two stations to get white noise and pressing it close to his ear, which makes him feel safe) and the policeman takes hold of his arm. He doesn't like being touched and he hits the policeman.

Chapter 13

The narrator tells us that this is not going to be a funny book. He tells a joke of his father's and says that the multi-layered nature of it made him feel confused and 'not nice like white noise'.

Chapter 17

The police officer arrests Christopher for hitting him. Christopher is told to get into the car, and they drive off to the station. Christopher notices that the car smells of 'hot plastic and aftershave and take-away chips'. As they drive Christopher watches the sky and sees the Milky Way. He explains what the Milky Way is and then explains why it is not light at night despite all the stars in the sky: the stars are all rushing away from one another as the universe expands and they will not rush towards earth until the universe stops expanding by which time humans will be long extinct.

Chapter 19

Christopher explains that he has decided to give his chapters prime numbers instead of the usual 'cardinal numbers 1,2,3'. He then explains how you work out prime numbers, revealing that no one has ever worked out a formula for calculating them - it would even take a computer years to work out whether a really really big number is a prime number or not. 'Prime numbers are what is left when you have taken all the patterns away' Christopher says and concedes that 'they are very logical but you could never work out the rules, even if you spent all your time thinking about them.'

Analysis

Chapter 11 is very clever because it sets up a crime scene which, if one was observing it from a little distance, would seem easily understood. A boy is seen with a dead dog, does not deny killing it and when the police approach him he cowers and then lashes out. It sets up a dual perspective: one has to get up close (as close as Christopher's narrative allows us into his head) to understand a situation; it is not good enough just observing from a distance. Christopher tells us that he likes police because 'the have uniforms and numbers and you know what they are meant to be doing.' Christopher doesn't like indecision and he likes to be sure of identity - this reminds us again of why he would not understand the Virginia Woolf quote. Christopher relates very literally to the world and doesn't analyze in the way you might expect.

Christopher does not grasp his situation - he does not seem to understand that he is being driven to the station for 'assaulting' the police officer. And yet he grasps the much bigger picture of the stars in relation to the earth and the concept of the universe expanding and contracting. The perspectives of this section are very interesting. Christopher looks up at the Milky Way and as he describes it, the perspective of him compared to the mathematical awesomeness of the universe is impressive – for him, there is security in the vastness and logic of the workings of the universe. The shifting focus from the 'hot plastic' to the stars is typical of the way Christopher thinks – his focus is detailed and absolute.

Christopher says he feels happiest and safe when he is listening to white noise – the noise between two radio frequencies - which is why he groans when the policeman asks him so many questions. He tries to replicate the noise created by a radio. He wants to block out the sounds of speech from the policeman, which he finds threatening because he cannot process the information. He also compares his mind to a bread maker – this relationship with machines and equating people to machines is common for Christopher. When he hears that his mother is going into hospital (p.29) he is pleased because he thinks he'll be able to visit the hospital which he likes because of the 'uniforms and machines'.

In this section Christopher explains why he has numbered his chapters in prime numbers: it is significant that he has chosen a pattern for his story which, as he explains, is the pattern left when all other patterns are taken away. It is almost as though this highly mathematically able child has actively sought to release himself from the confines of mathematical patterns to create something unique for his story.

Summary and Analysis of Section 3

Chapter 23

At the police station Christopher is asked to take the laces out of his shoes and to empty his pockets. He empties out a Swiss Army Knife with 13 attachments, a piece of string, a piece of wooden puzzle (of which he draws a diagram), 3 pellets of rat food for his rat Toby, £1.47, a red paperclip and a key for the front door. He screams when they try to take his watch off him because he needs to know exactly what time it is. Christopher answers some of their questions, telling the police men that his family consists of his Father (but Mother was dead), Uncle Terry and Grandma Burton. Christopher calculates that the police cell is 2 meters long by 2 meters wide by 2 meters high and wonders how he would escape if he was in a story. He thinks that he would wait for a sunny day and start a fire by reflecting the light in his glasses - he would escape when they evacuated his cell and if they didn't notice he would wee on the fire to put it out. Christopher wonders if Mrs Shears has told the police that he killed Wellington and wonders if she will go to prison for telling lies, which Christopher calls *slander*.

Chapter 29

Christopher explains that he finds people confusing for two main reasons: people talk with facial expressions as well as just words and people talk using metaphors. He says that metaphors are just confusing because you try and imagine a metaphor, for example an apple in someone's eye and it distracts you from what the person is actually talking about. Christopher says that his name is a metaphor and means *carrying Christ*. He says he does not want his name to mean the story where St Christopher carries Jesus across a river - he wants his name to mean him.

Chapter 31

Christopher's father arrives at the police station at 1.12am and is angry with policemen until 1.28am when he is let in to see Christopher. He holds up his right hand and spreads his fingers into a fan and Christopher's fingers touch his to show that he loves him and because Christopher does not like being hugged. They are taken to a room with an inspector. The inspector cautions Christopher for assaulting the policeman and asks whether Christopher killed the dog. Christopher and his father leave the station.

Chapter 37

Christopher explains why he can't lie. He says it is because 'there is only ever one thing which happened at a particular time and a particular place. And there are an infinite number of things which didn't happen at that time and that place.' He says if he opens up his imagination to something that he didn't do at that time then he would not be able to stop thinking of all the things he didn't do. He says that is why he doesn't like proper novels, because they are lies, and that **everything he has written is true**.

Analysis

Christopher likes the police cell: 'It was nice in the police cell. It was almost a perfect cube,' he says, describing the dimensions. Christopher feels comfortable in this room by himself and he starts imagining how he might escape if he were in a story. The irony of course is that he is in a story, albeit a story of his own creation. Mark Haddon endows Christopher with a real sense of authorship in this novel.

The cell could also be a metaphor for the blank pages of a book before the author starts writing. Within this cell, Christopher allows his imagination free reign as he conjures up a world from the serenity of the cell. Despite feeling comfortable in the cell, Christopher imagines ways of escaping, as though he is only too aware of how he is supposed to feel in such a situation, locked up as he is. Creativity is sometimes best expressed alone, with a blank canvas, and this is true for many writers - it is easy to imagine why the absence of external stimuli would be particularly inspiring for Christopher.

Christopher's language is very particular to him and he has a very specific relationship with it. He does not like metaphors because they distract from the story by forcing engagement with a totally different image. He also says that he wants his name to mean 'him'. Christopher clearly doesn't connect with anything that he sees as a lie: he relates very specifically and very directly with the information he receives, which is reflected in the way he tells his own story. Here we are made to think about the significance of language as far as writing and expressing yourself is concerned.

The authorial voice of the novel is so expressly Christopher's - Haddon is completely hidden within this character. In a way, Haddon is not only an author but also an actor. He has adopted the role of Christopher in order to tell this story.

Summary and Analysis of Section 4

Chapter 41

On the way home in the car Christopher's father asks Christopher to keep his nose out of other people's business and tells him he has to stay out of trouble. Christopher answers back that he didn't know he was going to get into trouble and that he hopes the policemen find Wellington's killer. Christopher's father bangs the steering wheel and shouts 'I said leave it, for God's sake'. Christopher knows he is angry because he is shouting. When he gets home he feeds Toby his rat, and when he goes down stairs to get orange squash before bed at 2.07am, he finds his father with tears coming out of his eyes as he is sitting drinking whisky and watching snooker. Christopher asks if he is sad about Wellington and he says 'You could very well say that.' Christopher goes back upstairs and says nothing else because he knows he prefers to be alone when he is sad.

Chapter 43

Christopher explains that his mother died two years ago. He came home from school and no one was there to answer the door so he found the key under the flowerpot and went in to make the Airfix Sherman Tank model he was building. His father came home later and asked if Christopher had seen his mother. When he said no he left the house for 2 1/2 hours. When he came back he told Christopher that he would not be seeing his mother for a while because she had a problem with her heart and she needed to rest without anyone being there. He did not look at Christopher when he said this and Christopher liked that because usually 'people look at you when they're talking to you. I know that they're working out what I'm thinking, but I can't tell what they're thinking. It is like being in a room with a one-way mirror in a spy film.' Christopher said that he wanted to make her a get well soon card and his father said that he'd take it the next day.

Chapter 47

In the bus on the way to school the next day Christopher sees 4 red cars in a row 'which meant that it was a **Good Day**. The psychologist at school had told him it wasn't very logical to think like this but Christopher argued that he likes things to be in a nice order and that people who work in offices are often happy when the sun is shining in the morning and sad when it is raining, even though the weather doesn't really affect them while they are sitting in an office. Christopher tells the psychologist that he would like to be an astronaut even though it was very difficult to become one. Terry at school tells him he will only get a job in the supermarket or at an animal sanctuary but his father tells him that Terry is only jealous. Christopher says that he is going to go to university and study maths or physics or maths and physics. On this good day, Christopher decides to try and find out who killed Wellington. Siobhan tells him that they're meant to be writing stories today and that is when Christopher starts writing his book.

Chapter 53

Two weeks after going into hospital, Christopher's mother died. Christopher did not go to the hospital but made her a get well card with nine red cars drawn in line on the front so that it would be a '**Super Super Good Day for Mother**'. Father told Christopher that she died of a heart attack but Christopher can't understand how - she was 38, very active and ate healthily. Mrs Shears came over and cooked Christopher and his father spaghetti, and then he beat her in scrabble 247 points to 134.

Analysis

This chapter begins 'Mother died two weeks later.' We assume that Christopher means that she died two weeks after going into hospital but it is not clear. His association with time depends on his version of the chronology of events. This is mirrored in his use of prime numbers to number his chapters.

It is still very early on in the novel and although most of us will have been seduced by Christopher's almost comforting way of thinking (he seems incapable of hiding what he thinks), we can already see the burden Christopher's unusual behavior has put on his father. There is a real tension here between the ways the two communicate. Christopher does not lie (as he tells us later on in the novel) and we are already seeing very clearly how incompatible that is to daily life. As his father, Ed is protective of Christopher, but the outburst at the beginning of this section shows that he is straining to manage and balance the relationship his son has with the world.

Symbolically, it is significant that Christopher is taken to the police station at the beginning of the novel. For the policemen, Christopher's groans and refusal to answer the question about whether or not he killed Wellington is enough for them to believe (along with the obvious reason that he is holding the dog when they find him) that he might have had something to do with its death. On the other hand, Christopher simply feels out of control and overwhelmed by the questions and it is only because policemen are used to people lying to get out of their crime that they become so quickly impatient and jump to conclusions. Christopher is literally and metaphorically locked up by the system: unable to communicate because what he has to say has already been projected on to him by the policemen: from their perspective, his behavior is suspicious and they cannot think outside of their habitual patterns of thought.

Haddon very cleverly signals to us that, although Christopher's behavior may seem strange to us, our own behavior is often strange but we have become so accustomed to it that we are blind to how illogical it can be. When the psychologist says it is illogical to equate red cars with good days, the reader sympathizes. And yet when it is pointed out by Christopher that people in offices often think it is going to be a good day when the sun is shining but miserable when it is not, nobody thinks that is illogical. Logically speaking, of course, he is right – the only difference between the two is that most of us feel happier in the sun and so it has become a culturally recognized feeling – not at all specific to the individual.

It is during this section that Siobhan suggests that Christopher write his story down, as part of the school assignment, and he tells us: 'And that is when I started writing this.' So, we feel as though we are a little behind Christopher because we have just got to the stage where he started writing the book and so there is a sense of urgency for us to keep reading because we know that he is always a little further ahead than us, a little closer to solving the puzzle.

Summary and Analysis of Section 5

Chapter 59

Despite Father's warnings to stay out of people's business, Christopher decides to find out who killed Wellington. Christopher admits that he does not always do what people tell him because their instructions often don't make sense. For instance 'people often say 'Be quiet', but they don't tell you how long to be quiet for.' Siobhan understands and gives him clear instructions about what to do and what not to do. That evening Christopher goes to Mrs Shears. She says she doesn't want to see him but he insists that he didn't kill Wellington and asks if she knows who did. She closes the door. Christopher waits until she thinks he has left and then climbs over the wall to her shed where the gardening tools are kept. The shed is padlocked but he notices, by looking through the window, that there is a fork in the shed which looks exactly the same as the one that was sticking out of Wellington: it had a green plastic handle and so did all the other tools. So Christopher decides that the fork must have belonged to Mrs Shears and that either she killed him (which he does not think is true) or it was someone who had the keys to her shed. He turns around and see Mrs Shears and she tells him to leave or she will call the police again. He leaves and feels happy because he is finding things out like a detective.

Chapter 61

When Christopher's mother died, Mrs Forbes at school said she had gone to heaven. Christopher says that is not true because heaven doesn't exist. When Reverend Peters once came to his school, Christopher asked him where heaven was. His response was 'It's not in our universe. It's another kind of place altogether.' Christopher does not accept this and gives him a scientific account of the only thing outside our universe that can be found if you go through a black hole. Reverend answers 'Well, when I say that heaven is outside the universe it's really just a manner of speaking. I suppose what it really means is that they are with God.' When Christopher asked where God was, he said that he'll discuss it on another day. Christopher explains that when you die you mix with the flowers and the plants when you are put into the ground. He explains that Mother was cremated and that he sometimes looks into the sky and thinks he can see 'molecules of Mother up there.'

Chapter 67

Saturday was the next day and Christopher decides to continue his detective work. He decides to go and ask some of the neighbors if they had seen anyone killing Wellington or had seen anything strange happening that night. He says he does not usually talk to strangers and that he doesn't really want to talk to strangers - not because he is scared because he could hit them hard, like he did when Sarah pulled his hair and he knocked her into a concussion and she was sent to Accident and Emergency - but because he doesn't like people he's never met before. At school he spends weeks watching new members of staff until he feels safe and doesn't have to watch them all the time. He speaks to the old lady, Mrs Alexander at number 39. She offers Christopher squash and biscuits, but she is in the house for six minutes and Christopher starts worrying about whether she was telling the truth or whether she was calling the police. So he walks away and then has a thought. The most sensible reason he could think that someone would have killed Wellington was to make Mrs Shears sad and the only person he could think would want to make Mrs Shears sad was Mr Shears, who moved out of the house two years ago. Christopher deduces that since Mr Shears did not want to live with Mrs Shears anymore, 'he probably hated her and he might have come back and killed her dog to make her sad.'

Chapter 71

Christopher says that all the children at his school are stupid but that he's been told that he should say that they have learning difficulties or special needs. He says that he is going to prove that he is not stupid by taking A level Maths next month and by getting an A grade. He is the first pupil to take an A level at the school and the headmistress didn't want him to take it at first because she had they didn't have the facilities and she didn't want Christopher to be treated differently because then everyone would want to be treated differently. Christopher's father complained and said that he would pay the £50 for an invigilator and she agreed. Christopher says that after he has taken A level Maths he is going to take A level Further Maths and Physics and then go to university. He will have to go to a university away from his home town, Swindon because there isn't one in Swindon, but he says that would suit his father fine because then they could both move. When he has done his degree he will be able to get a job and earn money to pay for a cook and cleaner or he will marry a lady who will look after him and will be his companion.

Analysis

It is interesting, in light of what we find out at the end of the novel, that there is a whole chapter dedicated to death and to where Christopher's mother went when she died. In some ways there is a real irony to this because his thoughts about his mother's death are, in Christopher's worldview, a lie, because she hasn't actually died. But he does not know that yet. Again, I think this points to the power of storytelling: it is a big part of Christopher's life that his mother is dead and that fact really colors his vision of the world – so, the way each of us views the world is not so much based on fact but on what we think is happening in our lives.

Christopher's relationship with the universe is very spiritual even though he hasn't given his feelings a label. As he says early on in this section, 'I do not always do what I am told. And this is because when people tell you what to do it is usually confusing and does not make sense.' This is true of not only what people tell you to do, but also of what people tell you. It is important to note that the Reverend postpones the conversation with Christopher about where God is located because he does not have an answer himself: Christopher's need to understand – which is a need many children have – cannot accept or accommodate the Reverend's woolly answers and as a result he is quite obviously exposed.

It is also very important for the structure of the story that Christopher does not listen to his father's words of warning about finding Wellington's killer; if he had, there would be no novel. The courage to follow your own beliefs and instincts until you are fully persuaded by another has meant that we have a novel to read – it has brought to life this whole experience. Haddon seems to imply that the opposite is deadly, and stops you from being an individual.

It is significant that Christopher thinks the people in his class are stupid because it at once differentiates the people within his school and makes sure that none of us fall into the trap of seeing all the pupils at Christopher's school in the same way. It is made very clear – and is very clear from the novel – that Christopher is highly intelligent and unique, even if he is incapable of functioning in a mainstream school.

Summary and Analysis of Section 6

Chapter 73

Christopher explains that his Mother and Father used to argue a lot due to the stress of looking after someone with Behavioral Problems. He explains that he has grown out of most of his Behavioral Problems and lists them. The list includes: 'Not liking being touched', 'Smashing things when I am angry or confused', 'Not eating good if different sorts of food are touching each other', 'Saying things that other people think are rude'. Mother and Father sometimes used to shout at Christopher - Mother saying 'You are going to drive me into an early grave.'

Chapter 79

When Christopher gets home his Father is sitting at the table where he had laid the baked beans, broccoli and two slices of ham (which aren't touching) and he tells Christopher that he has recently had a call from Mrs Shears. Christopher tells his father that he thinks Mr Shears killed Wellington and his father slams his hand down and says 'I will not have that man's name mentioned in my house...That man is evil.' He asks Christopher to promise not to carry on with his investigation and Christopher promises.

Chapter 83

Christopher explains that he would love to be an astronaut and that he would be very good at the job: He is intelligent, he understands how machines work, he likes being on his own in tiny spaces, he would be happy because there are no yellow or brown things in a spacecraft (and he doesn't like yellow or brown things), he would be able to talk to other people from Mission Control who wouldn't be like strangers, and he would be able to look out at the stars and know that there was nobody around him for hundreds of miles. Ideally, he'd love to take his rat Toby with him.

Chapter 89

The next day at school Christopher tells Siobhan that his father has told him to stop 'detecting'. Therefore the book he was writing is finished. Siobhan tells him that he should be pleased that he has written a book at all but Christopher says it cannot be a proper book because he never found out who the murderer was. Siobhan tells Christopher that life is like that: there are lots of murders unsolved and lots of murderers who aren't caught. Christopher doesn't like this idea and he worries about bumping into the murderer at night. He then asks Siobhan why his father said that Mr Shears was evil and tells her that he thinks Mr Shears is a suspect. Siobhan cannot answer Christopher. The next two days, Christopher sees 4 yellow cars, making them Black Days. On the third day he travels to school with his eyes closed - because, after two Black Days in a row, he is 'allowed to do that.'

Analysis

It is significant that Christopher wants to be an astronaut. He wants to work in a vehicle that takes him as far away from earth as humans can possibly go. This shows how fundamentally distanced he feels from the world and the way it works and shows the relationship he would prefer to have with it: as though it were a computer game.

For the reader, there is definitely something suspicious about the fact that Christopher's father became so agitated about Mr Shears, and about the fact that Mrs Shears is no longer a friend of the family. We can see that there is clearly something that is being hidden from Christopher, but Christopher cannot read the very clues he puts before us - he relates what he sees, but he cannot parse the emotional vocabulary.

Most of the things that Christopher lists under his behavioral problems are problems with communicating. His parents want to touch him to communicate affection but he does not like to be touched, and when he cannot communicate effectively (as when 'angry or confused'), he 'smashes things' and he says things 'that other people think are rude'.

Summary and Analysis of Section 7

Chapter 97

Five days later Christopher sees five red cars in a row, which meant it was going to be a **Super Good Day**. At the shop at the end of his road after school Christopher bumps into Mrs Alexander. Christopher avoids talking to her so as not to get into any trouble but after exchanging a few words he considers that nothing 'super' had happened yet and that talking to Mrs Alexander may well be the special thing that was going to happen that day.

Thinking through the list of things his father forbade him to do, Christopher reasons that talking to Mrs Alexander does not break any of the rules. He asks her 'Do you know Mr Shears?'

Mrs Alexander asks Christopher why he is so interested in Mr Shears - she wonders if it is because of Wellington. She says it is best not to talk about Mr Shears and that it will upset Christopher's father and that Christopher knows why his father doesn't like Mr Shears. Christopher doesn't understand and asks Mrs Alexander why his father doesn't like Mr Shears. Worried that she has already said too much and that Christopher will ask his father what she meant, Mrs Alexander tells Christopher the truth and makes him promise he won't tell his father she told him. Before she died, Christopher's mother was having an affair with Mr Shears.

Chapter 101

In this chapter, Christopher presents a mathematical problem. He tells of how in a magazine in America there was a column called *Ask Marilyn*, written by a woman with the highest IQ in the world. In 1990 a question was sent to Marilyn: on a game show program there are three doors. Behind one door there is a car, behind the other two there are goats. You pick one door and another opens, revealing a goat. You are asked whether you want to change your mind about the two unopened doors. Marilyn argues that you should always change your mind and pick the final door as there is a two in three chance that the car will be behind that.

Lots of people wrote in to complain that she was wrong and she explained why she was not. Intuition would say that there is a 50% chance that the car will be behind the original door chosen but logic states that there is a one third chance that it will be behind the original.

This is why Christopher thinks logic is more reliable than intuition for working out problems in life.

Chapter 103

Christopher returns home from his trip to the shop where he bumped into Mrs Alexander. The maintenance mann is drinking beer and watching TV with his father.

Christopher tells us that Siobhan said that it was important to include description in a book so that people can imagine the picture in their heads. Christopher goes out into the garden with the intention of 'doing a description' but is only interested in the sky, which he describes in detail.

Chapter 107

The Hound of the Baskervilles is Christopher's favorite book and he recaps the story. Christopher like Sherlock Holmes because he notices the kind of things that Christopher notices. Christopher quotes Dr Watson's observation of Sherlock Holmes from the book: *...his mind...was busy in endeavoring to frame some scheme into which all these strange and apparently disconnected episodes could be fitted.* Christopher says that is what he is trying to do by writing the book.

Analysis

The first part of the jigsaw puzzle is revealed, although we still believe that Christopher's mother is dead.

Christopher believes that the day will be a good one because he sees five red cars in a row. His own sense of order is like a religion – if it is a super day then maybe the signs are indicating to him that Mrs Alexander is a useful person to speak to.

It is interesting that Christopher has his own almost religious symbols: to him, five red cars definitely means it is going to be a super day - knowing that he decides he will risk speaking to Mrs Alexander. In a way his decision here is based on what he sees as a logical decision that something super will happen and that that may well be the conversation with Mrs Alexander.

When Mrs Alexander tells Christopher not to talk about Mr Shears because he knows it will upset his father we realize that Christopher's mystery goes a lot deeper than he knows: there are clearly secrets that have been kept from him and as a result the reader must think that it is possible that there are people who know who killed Wellington. At this stage however, Mrs Alexander holds true to the fact that Christopher's mother is dead - how much do we believe this? Was Mrs Alexander telling what she believed to be the truth? Who is to be believed and who is acting?

The mathematical problem Christopher relates shows his relationship with the world as one based on logic and not feeling. This of course it exactly how the book is written - a logical step by step account trying to ascertain who killed Wellington. The story he relates about the magazine columnist is quite true - the problem was mentioned in the "Ask Marilyn" column of *Parade* in 1990, and due to the incredible reader response an unprecedented four columns were given to publishing a mathematical explanation. The puzzle is most commonly known as the Monty Hall Problem, after the host of the game show "Let's Make A Deal" in which, yes, Monty Hall gave players a choice between doors containing cars and goats.

Christopher is interested in describing the sky because it takes him further away from earth. Again we have a kind of commentary through Siobhan, who gives instructions on how to write a novel, which Christopher sporadically follow. Siobhan's advice reads as ridiculous in this context, because Christopher's novel is most compelling when he follows his own way of viewing the world, rather than adhering to convention. The sky description doesn't so much make us paint a picture as tell us about Christopher and the way he sees things.

Summary and Analysis of Section 8

Chapter 109

Christopher tells us that he wrote some more of his book the night before and that he showed it to Siobhan the next day. She asked him if he was sad about the conversation he'd had with Mrs Alexander and that he could talk to her about it if he ever did feel sad. Christopher says that, since his mother is dead and Mr Shears isn't around, it would be stupid to be sad about something that doesn't exist.

Chapter 113

Christopher explains how his memory works. He says it is like a DVD that you can rewind to any point and replay the situation exactly - so long as it was after he was four years old, he clarifies, because that was when he started looking at things properly. He tells us about a scene with him and his mother in Cornwall when he was nine in 1992. To recognize someone he does not know he does a **Search** through his memories to see if he's seen their walk or glasses or hair before. He says he has pictures in his head of things that happened but can't understand the pictures people make up in their heads of things that haven't happened.

Chapter 127

Christopher gets home before his father and puts his things on the kitchen table (including his book) and sits in the living room to watch a *Blue Planet* video. When his father comes home at 5.48pm he is in a good mood but goes to the kitchen and stays there until 5.54pm, when he reemerges with Christopher's book in hand. He is quiet to start, so Christopher doesn't know that he's angry, but he soon starts shouting about the conversation Christopher had with Mrs Alexander. He grabs Christopher (which he has never done before), who hits him back. At this point Christopher's memories stop and he only remembers sitting against the wall with blood on his right hand. His father leaves for the garden, still with the book in his hand, and puts it in the bin.

Chapter 131

Christopher states some reasons why he hates the colors yellow and brown. He recalls that Mrs Forbes said it was silly to hate yellow and brown but that Siobhan had said that she shouldn't say things like that because everyone had favorite colors. Christopher does say he thinks it is silly in a way but says that in life you have to make decisions and if you didn't you would 'never do anything because you would spend all your time choosing between things you could do.'

Chapter 137

The next day Christopher's father says he's sorry for hitting him and says he will take Christopher to Twycross Zoo to show that he really was sorry. At the cafe at lunch, Christopher's father apologizes again and tells Christopher how much he loves him. Then Christopher draws a map of the zoo from memory.

Chapter 139

Christopher tells the story of *The Case of the Cottingley Fairies* where, in 1917, two cousins - one nine and one sixteen - took photographs of the fairies they used to play with. People believed the photographs for years but Christopher says it is stupid and that the cousins admitted it was a fake in 1981.

Chapter 149

After school on Monday - when Siobhan had questioned Christopher about his bruised face and asked if he was scared to go home - Christopher went into the bin in the garden to look for his book. He missed it and liked having a project. He couldn't find it there, so he looked around the house. He looked in his father's room, even though he had said that Christopher shouldn't mess with anything in there. Christopher determines to move everything back where it was so he will never know. He finds his book in a shirt box in the cupboard and doesn't know what to do because if he moves it his father will know he had been messing around.

Christopher hears his father come home and makes a quick decision - he will leave the book there and copy information out of it when necessary when his father is not home. Just then he notices a letter addressed to him. He takes the letter and quietly leaves his father's room, hides the letter under his mattress, and goes downstairs to have dinner with his father.

When he goes back up to his room he opens the letter. It is from his mother, writing from London. It is dated a year and a half after she died.

Christopher says that it must be a letter to another Christopher from his mother, and that he was in the middle of another mystery.

Chapter 151

In this chapter Christopher explains that there are mysteries for which we have no answer, but science will one day explain all. Lightening was a mystery before they realized it was electricity, and one day ghosts will be explained too.

Analysis:

When Christopher describes his memory as a DVD player, we realize that he is embodied in the novel - we hold a copy of his mind, the DVD that it plays back. We can turn back the pages at whatever point to replay any scenes. Christopher grants us his power for replaying situations exactly, putting us in his shoes.

When Christopher and his father have a fight, his memory is significantly wiped out - that of course is when the book is thrown away. His connection with the outside world is momentarily halted and it seems no coincidence that this is precisely the time when the book is discovered by his father and thrown away. His connection with the outside world is through his book and they have almost become one and the same.

Christopher here is distinguishing between real and fake, in a novel primarily about deceit. Although Christopher understands very clearly that the fairies are a fake he has not yet uncovered the lies happening right before him. It also points to how convincing art can be - the photographs were thought of as real in the way that this novel is presented as non-fiction.

Christopher finds himself in a mini mystery when he is searching for his book and this mystery leads him to a truth long hidden: his mother is still alive and living in London. Suddenly we have found ourselves in a far more vital mystery than that of the dog - we want to look back and see what actually happened to his mother. Because Christopher has been lied to and we see the world from his eyes, we feel equally betrayed.

When Christopher first finds his mother's letters to him, he cannot believe that they are what they appear to be - so much so that he believes he has intercepted a letter meant for a different Christopher. When faced with contradictory facts, Christopher's logical brain presents the simplest solution to arrange them - a lie is not an option, because he is incapable of conceiving of willful deceit.

Summary and Analysis of Section 9

Chapter 157

It is six days before Christopher can go in his father's shirt box again. On the fifth day it rains very hard and Christopher watches the water falling out of his window.

On the sixth day Christopher's father is called out on an emergency - there has been a flood - so Christopher goes to the shirt box.

There are 43 letters in total - all addressed to Christopher.

In one letter his mother writes about happy times when they bought Christopher a train set and he loved it. In the second letter his mother explains in some detail why she left him. She says she was hot tempered and not as good as his father at looking after him. She fell in love with Eileen's Roger because she was lonely and he was lonely, and when he asked her to move to London with him she agreed, because she thought it would be better for everyone. In the third she writes that she hopes he got the present she sent.

After the forth letter Christopher feels giddy and sick that his father lied to him that his mother was dead. He lies in bed curled up. Christopher doesn't remember much after that - just waking up after dark with vomit on his bed.

His father walks in, realizes what's happened and apologizes and apologizes. Christopher is quiet and feels him touching his shoulder but he doesn't mind. When he lifts Christopher on to the bed to take his clothes off and put him in the bath, he doesn't mind either.

Chapter 163

Christopher compares how the mind works and how computers work

Chapter 167

After Christopher's father gives him a bath, he is very open with Christopher and says that he can trust him and that he is sorry. He says that he was only lying to protect him, but that from now on he would always be honest. He tells Christopher that he was the one who killed Wellington. He and Eileen had been getting on really well after his mother left and he thought that one day they might all move in together, but he and Eileen had fights. After one really horrible one where she said horrible things, she threw him out and the dog came after him, and that's when all the bad feelings over the last two years came bubbling up.

Christopher is scared when he hears this and waits for his father to fall asleep in the living room. He takes his Swiss army knife and Toby, puts on his coat, and goes out of the house. He squeezes between the wall of the shed and the fence and thinks what to do next.

Chapter 173

From his hiding place, Christopher watches the stars and notes the different constellations.

Analysis:

This section is the turning point of the novel. It is through reading that Christopher uncovers the biggest secret of all: Haddon really celebrates the power of communication through the written word. In the way that Christopher has enlightened us about how he sees the world by writing his story, his mother's letters shed light on the mystery that has been puzzling him. Note that Christopher's spelling is great but his mum's isn't!

The original mystery of Wellington actually pointed to a fundamental mystery about Christopher's own life - what began as trivial became profound. Structurally, this novel is not too distant from classical tragedy. Think of Oedipus, who, searching out the riddle of the Sphinx, instead learns a fundamental secret about his own life that had previously been hidden from him. Classical tragedy also brings the fall of the house, and here too the revelation destroys a home - Christopher no longer feels like his father's house is his home, and he begins his long journey to find his mother.

Christopher is jolted out of his pattern of reacting violently to touch, because of the extraordinary discovery he has made. A non-autistic child might have responded with uncharacteristic calmness when faced with such a shock, and here Christopher responds with uncharacteristic passivity. There is a very telling quote in chapter 167 where, apologizing and explaining to him, Christopher's father says: 'Life is difficult, you know. It's bloody hard telling the truth all the time.' In actual fact, Christopher finds the difficulty of life to be the exact opposite – he seems to find it impossible to lie. In chapter 167 Christopher compares his mind to a computer and when his father apologizes and he says nothing, it is almost as though his whole being is re-booting in order to process this shocking information.

As far as Christopher is concerned his father is a murderer, and he must escape. The image of Christopher's father killing the dog is made to sound almost cartoon-like and totally removed; yet killing a dog with a garden fork is extremely gruesome and brutal. Christopher's fear after finding out about Wellington is totally understandable - it is as though his father has been revealed as a stranger. If his father has killed Wellington and lied about his mother, then Christopher cannot trust him at all.

Summary and Analysis of Section 10

Chapter 179

Christopher hides until dawn, and when he hears his father looking for him in the morning, he squeezed himself between the wall of the shed and the fence and covers himself with the fertilizer sack. When his father leaves in the van, he knows it is safe to come out. He knew he couldn't live with his father anymore so he decides to live with Mrs Shears, but she doesn't answer the door when he knocks.

He decides that going to live with Mother in London was the best option. He knocks on Mrs Alexander's door and asks her to look after Toby, and tells her where he is going and why. Mrs Alexander tries to persuade him to come in and talk, and she suggests ringing his father. Christopher runs away, breaking into his own house. After picking up enough provisions for himself and Toby, he sets off for the train to London.

Chapter 181

Christopher explains that the reason why he doesn't like new places is because he notices everything and when you notice everything in a new place your head feels full and you sometimes feel as though you need to reboot it, like when you press CTRL, ALT and DEL on the computer.

Chapter 191

At the train station, Christopher feels 'giddy and sick' because of all the new things he notices and because of all the people walking around. Christopher calms himself down by - among other things - distracting himself with math problems, putting his hands over his ears and pretending he is in a computer game. After a while a policeman comes up to him and tells Christopher that he has been there for two and a half hours and was acting like he was in a trance. Christopher feels safer with the policeman and answers all of his questions. The policeman takes him to the ATM to get money for the train, and shows him where to get his ticket. Christopher then walks through a difficult underpass and boards the train.

Chapter 193

Christopher explains why he likes timetables and that on weekends he makes a timetable for himself so that he knows what is going to happen. He says he likes them because 'they make sure you don't get lost in time.'

Analysis:

For the first time in the novel, the mystery is not Christopher's to solve, but

Christopher's to pose; he now has all the answers, and everyone back home must figure out where he has gone. Christopher is no longer the detective, but the detected.

This is the first time Christopher is outside his hometown. This is the second time we see Christopher with a policeman and it is interesting that his views about them have not been tainted by the previous experience: Christopher is pleased to see him because he still associates policemen with order, despite his negative recent encounter.

Summary and Analysis of Section 11

Chapter 179

Christopher hides until dawn, and when he hears his father looking for him in the morning, he squeezed himself between the wall of the shed and the fence and covers himself with the fertilizer sack. When his father leaves in the van, he knows it is safe to come out. He knew he couldn't live with his father anymore so he decides to live with Mrs Shears, but she doesn't answer the door when he knocks.

He decides that going to live with Mother in London was the best option. He knocks on Mrs Alexander's door and asks her to look after Toby, and tells her where he is going and why. Mrs Alexander tries to persuade him to come in and talk, and she suggests ringing his father. Christopher runs away, breaking into his own house. After picking up enough provisions for himself and Toby, he sets off for the train to London.

Chapter 181

Christopher explains that the reason why he doesn't like new places is because he notices everything and when you notice everything in a new place your head feels full and you sometimes feel as though you need to reboot it, like when you press CTRL, ALT and DEL on the computer.

Chapter 191

At the train station, Christopher feels 'giddy and sick' because of all the new things he notices and because of all the people walking around. Christopher calms himself down by - among other things - distracting himself with math problems, putting his hands over his ears and pretending he is in a computer game. After a while a policeman comes up to him and tells Christopher that he has been there for two and a half hours and was acting like he was in a trance. Christopher feels safer with the policeman and answers all of his questions. The policeman takes him to the ATM to get money for the train, and shows him where to get his ticket. Christopher then walks through a difficult underpass and boards the train.

Chapter 193

Christopher explains why he likes timetables and that on weekends he makes a timetable for himself so that he knows what is going to happen. He says he likes them because 'they make sure you don't get lost in time.'

Chapter 197

On the train, Christopher keeps still in an attempt to forget that he is in a train carriage with lots of people. The policeman calls his name and asks him to come with him to meet his father. Christopher doesn't want to go and screams when the policeman tries to touch him. Then the train starts and the policeman is annoyed that he didn't get Christopher off the train in time. They sit down and after a while Christopher goes to the toilet - the policeman tells him he's watching him so he shouldn't try to escape. Near the toilet, Christopher notices a cupboard like one at home, where Christopher used to hide to feel safe. He climbs in and shuts the door. When the train stops at the next station, the policeman frantically looks for Christopher but can't find him - he gets off the train and leaves Christopher behind.

Chapter 199

Christopher explains why it is not so surprising that there are humans in the world and that if you think logically you can work out why everything in the world has happened. He uses this as evidence that there is no God.

Chapter 211

The train stops. Christopher decides to get off the shelf. The policeman had left and had taken his bag. Christopher gets off the train, and to hide from the noisy station he kneels on the ground for awhile. A man goes to fetch a policeman, and Christopher instead finds his way to the entrance to the London Underground. He watches people for a while from the photobooth in the station to learn how to buy a ticket and insert it into the machine. In the Underground, Christopher moans as the train screeches in, not knowing what was causing the noise - he can do nothing because the sound was hurting so much.

Chapter 223

Christopher describes the advertisement on the wall of the train station, because Siobhan had said that he should include descriptions in his story.

Christopher says that you don't need to see new things by going traveling - you just need to look at the earth under a microscope.

Analysis:

For the first time in the novel, the mystery is not Christopher's to solve, but Christopher's to pose; he now has all the answers, and everyone back home must figure out where he has gone. Christopher is no longer the detective, but the detected.

This is the first time Christopher is outside his hometown. This is the second time we see Christopher with a policeman and it is interesting that his views about them have not been tainted by the previous experience: Christopher is pleased to see him because he still associates policemen with order, despite his negative recent encounter.

Christopher's sole goal is to get to his mother in London. When he hides in the cupboard and evades the police officer, though, his aim is not in losing the police but just in feeling separated and safe. It becomes almost a farce as the grown-up characters fail to foresee how Christopher will respond to these new situations - he outsmarts the police not through cleverness, but just through behaving differently in the world than they expect.

Christopher describes his experience in the train station as though it were a computer game. He uses the game analogy to compartmentalize his observations and make them less threatening. The result is that we are shown the way our daily world can in fact be processed as a series of steps, each of which needs to be learned. To function, Christopher must draw maps and use equations and walk along an invisible red line from point A to point B. We are made to understand just how difficult navigating the world can be for the differently-abled.

Throughout the book, Christopher has included a fair number of charts and maps to illustrate his points. This section includes an even greater number of non-prose artifacts and examples. Not only does he write out his math problems, but he also shows us the patterns of the carpeting and the signs in the tube station. This shows that Christopher is being exposed to a huge range of new sensory input, which he must describe in order to process. It also shows us how much more work he needs to do to compartmentalize this new environment.

Summary and Analysis of Section 12

Chapter 227

Still scared in the station, Christopher notices that Toby is missing. He looks for him and sees him on the tracks, so he jumps off the platform and follows Toby. A man on the platform tells him to get out but Christopher keeps trying to reach Toby and as he does, he hears the sound of the train. The man helps him on to the platform just in time.

Christopher boards the next train and gets off at Willesden Junction. He buys a map guide so that he can find Chapter Road, and when he gets to 451c Chapter Road his mother isn't in, so he waits. Christopher is cold and wet, and his mother runs a bath for him. His mother pleads with Christopher to allow her to just hold his hand, but he refuses. He tells her that his father said she was dead and that he never got any of her letters.

A policeman arrives and asks Christopher questions: had he run away and was this his mother? He answers yes, and when he tells them he wants to live with his mother, they leave. Christopher goes to sleep but wakes up at 2.31am and hears his father and mother and Roger shouting. After several angry words Christopher's father comes into Christopher's room and says he's sorry and holds out his right hand, spreading his fingers out in a fan with tears dripping off his face. But Christopher is frightened and doesn't meet fingers with him. Then a policeman takes Christopher's father out of the flat and Christopher goes back to sleep.

Chapter 229

Christopher describes a recurring dream, in which a virus has killed most of the planet and the only survivors are those who prefer to stay away from other people, like him. This is a happy dream. With all the other people gone, Christopher can do what he pleases and explore the world without worrying about other people trying to talk to him or touch him.

Chapter 233

The next day Christopher remembers that he has to go back to Swindon to sit his Maths A-level, but he doesn't want to see his father. His mother has lost her job as well. One night Mr Shears comes into Christopher's room and says 'You think you're so fucking clever, don't you? Don't you ever think about other people?'

The next morning Christopher and his mother pack the car and drive to Swindon. When they get to the house in Swidon, Christopher's parents argue, and his father goes to stay with a friend. The school arranges for the invigilator to come in so Christopher can sit his A-level, even though he is very tired. Soon Christopher's mother gets a job, and the two of them move into a room in a big house.

Christopher still won't talk to his father even though he has to stay in his house from 3.49 until his mother picks him up after work at 5.30. Christopher's father proposes that they do a project together, so he can show Christopher that he can be trusted. He reveals a golden retriever puppy - the puppy will be Christopher's if he goes to his father's house to walk it. Christopher begins spending more time at his father's and starts planning things for the future: to do further math A-level next year, then physics A-level the year after, then get a first class honors degree and then be a scientist. He knows he can do this because he solved the mystery, because he went to London on his own and because he wrote a book.

Analysis:

Losing Toby is the climax of the whole story. Although clearly Christopher will survive the jump on to the train tracks (as he is narrating the story), Haddon builds remarkable suspense. It is also notable that despite Christopher's difficulty connecting to other humans, he feels so strongly responsible for his pet rat that he will risk his life to find him. The key, of course, is that Christopher doesn't realize he is risking his life. His thinking is too compartmentalized - all he knows is that Toby is on the tracks, and therefore he should go on to the tracks to fetch him.

At the end of the novel Ed buys his son a puppy: there is renewal at the end of the novel where there was death at the start. Mr Shears shows himself to be as ignorant and insensitive as his previous wife and there is a symmetry to the whole story that must be pleasing to the narrator.

One of the most devastating moments in the novel is when Christopher refuses to let his mother hold his hand. She hasn't seen her son for two years, and he has just survived a truly terrifying voyage to reach her. And yet she cannot satisfy her maternal instinct to cuddle him. She cannot even hold his hand. Most people express their love through touch, but Christopher is incapable of this emotional experience, even as he understands it rationally. Therefore, those who truly love him, like his mother, are forced to work within his comfort range. And so the mother cannot hold her child. This moment vividly captures the difficulty of raising a differently-abled child.

The novel ends on a note of total happiness and hope. Not only has Christopher found his mother and normalized relations with his father, but he has also begun to learn to express his emotions in a way that is understandable by most people. He has written this book, which he knows is a huge accomplishment. But he also notes that his A level made him feel glad by drawing a smiley face - perhaps he doesn't smile himself, but he can identify his feeling with a facial expression. He has made progress.

Suggested Essay Questions

1. **How significant is it to the novel that Christopher has learning difficulties?**

Think about how significant Christopher's perspective is to how the story is and to its structure. What is Haddon able to conceal/reveal by using Christopher? What light does it shed on the other characters in the novel, and on mankind in general? Discuss how Christopher's overcoming of his particular challenges adds another layer of drama to the actual plot of the story.

2. **What is Siobhan's role in the novel?**

Think about her role in how Christopher's story unfolds - it is she who encourages him to write the novel and her perspective on novel writing comes up throughout. Does her voice give us any comment on novel writing in general? What is her purpose? Would this novel exist at all without her? In a way, she is Haddon's true authorial voice poking through the facade of Christopher's narration.

3. **Discuss the meta fictional elements of this novel and why they are significant**

Christopher states directly that he intends to write a mystery novel, and the tropes of the classic mystery are explained to us even as he does his detecting. But aside from the mystery Christopher sets out to solve, he also ends up being part of a larger mystery not of his design. How much control does Christopher have over the events that unfold and how are h feelings documented in the novel we are reading?

4. **Discuss the first person narrative employed by Haddon to portray the novel from Christopher's perspective.**

Discuss other novels written in the first person - how is it used differently here? Does it work well in this novel? Why? Perhaps talk about how the other characters may feel removed from Christopher because of his condition and relationship with the world and discuss how the structure and the technique of writing in this novel comments on that. Compare to other novels with developmentally disabled narrators, such as *Flowers for Algernon* and *The Sound and The Fury*.

5. **Discuss Christopher's relationship with space**

You will need to have specific examples for the question: find all the examples where he talks about the sky and about space and discuss the relevance of this in relation to the novel as a whole. Does it reflect Christopher's ambition and intelligence? Does it reflect man's advancement in science? Why does the sky and the stars make him feel calm? Relate these points to his other habits and routines. How does this information inform the telling of the novel?

6. **Is there any way in which *The Curious Incident of the Dog in the Night-time* could be described as a classical tragedy? Discuss.**

Compare Christopher's lack of knowledge with the lack of knowledge often found in tragedies. Oedipus tries to end the plague of infertility that hits Thebes and when the oracle tells Creon that King Laius' murderer must be brought to justice in order for the pestilence to cease, Oedipus looks elsewhere for the murderer. Oedipus is 'detecting' and as he does, he realizes that the answer to the mystery is in his own house. The same is true for Christopher. How far does this constitute a tragedy, and what difference does it make that Christopher's perspective is an unusual one?

7. **Do you think this novel is more naturally a children's novel?**

This answer asks for you to be creative. You must discuss literary terms, you must address the style of the writing and you must point out what effect this has on the reader. Is it a 'simple' novel? Does it deal with complex issues? If yes, how does it deal with these issues? What is the tone of the novel and how does the writer engage his reader. How do we empathise with Christopher?

8. **How far do you think Christopher's condition limits or enlightens his perspective on life?**

This is a broad question and one which requires specific detail. Identify specific scenes in which Christopher behaves unusually according to generally accepted patterns of behavior, and discuss whether these incidents allow him to see more clearly or limit his understanding. The fact that he doesn't realize his mother is alive may be one example, but also address that many other characters are inveigled as well. Compare Christopher's philosophy of truth-telling to his father's.

9. **How does Haddon build tension in this novel?**

Focus on technical details in terms of the structure of the novel and the writing style - what information does he hide from Christopher, so that it will be revealed to us at a more useful juncture. Also incorporate a personal response. Examples may include Christopher losing Toby on the tube tracks, or a more general level of tension throughout the novel in terms of his detective work.

10. **Does this novel fulfill expectations that Christopher builds at the start by labeling it a 'detective novel'?**

First you may want to define a 'detective novel', perhaps using examples from other novels (a reference to Sherlock Holmes would obviously be very helpful). Analyze the structure of *the Curious Incident of the Dog in the Night-time* and assess how it progresses, builds tension and keeps our interest. How significant is it that Christopher solves one mystery and finds another. How far does the fact that it is all documented in this novel in real time create a sense of immediacy?

The "idiot-savant" as narrator

Christopher is part of a long literary tradition of first-person narrators with unreliable or otherwise compromised ways of telling their story. Although Haddon's novel may seem new and unique in structure, it is also a modern example of a 20th century literary form.

Christopher is what was once known as an idiot-savant. He has difficulty with things that should be easy, like reading emotions, and finds easy things that should be difficult, like remembering exact details. It is a not uncommon psychological phenomenon that people with autism spectrum disorders and other developmental and cognitive disabilities will show extreme proficiency in one or more isolated skills. Christopher manifests a good deal of these savant characteristics, and his autism is mild enough to allow him to be extremely high functioning - these two characteristics combine to make him an excellent narrator.

He is not dissimilar in this way from his hero, Sherlock Holmes. Although Holmes is not a narrator (his stories are narrated by his colleague Dr. Watson), he is also extraordinarily gifted at isolated skills - and has a very hard time understanding emotions and interacting with people in a normal way. In the case of Holmes, the character is so brilliant that he can overcome his limitations through excellent acting and deduction of patterns, but one can see why Christopher so identifies with his fictional hero.

But Christopher has several other more direct antecedents. One of the most famous idiot-savants is Raymond Babbitt in the film "Rainman," as portrayed by Dustin Hoffman. Raymond, like Christopher, is high-functioning autistic with similar savant characteristics, such as performing complex calculations in his head. The film was responsible for bringing autism to greater attention in American culture. It is understandable while Raymond and Christopher are both more sympathetic to normally-abled audiences and readers because of their savant characteristics, but as a result many people have skewed expectations of people with autism spectrum disorders.

Another important antecedent is Charlie in *Flowers for Algernon*. This 1966 novel had the same gimmick as *Curious Incident* - it was being written in real time by its narrator, in this case a severely developmentally disabled man named Charlie. But Charlie was undergoing a radical (and fictional) treatment which drastically increased his IQ, and as his journals progress he becomes more and more intelligent. With Charlie, the author Daniel Keyes was able to show us the unfamiliar perspectives of individuals at both extremes of the IQ bell curve, all in the same character.

But some disabled narrators are successful even without characteristics of brilliance. In Faulkner's *The Sound and the Fury*, the severely developmentally disabled Benjy

Compton narrates a quarter of the novel. The prose in this section is extremely difficult to penetrate, due to its stream-of-consciousness style and the difficulty of identifying with Benjy. But it has been extremely influential in modern literary fiction.

On the flip side, there are many brilliant narrators whose disability is not cognitive or developmental, but physical. Helen Keller was one of the most remarkable minds of the 20th century, but from the age of 19 months was completely deafblind. Her books, such as *The Story of My Life*, give the reader an introduction to how a deafblind person perceives the world, much as Christopher and Charlie introduce us to their perception of the world, but with the lucidity of a brilliant writer.

Author of ClassicNote and Sources

Zara Walters, author of ClassicNote. Completed on March 30, 2011, copyright held by GradeSaver.

Updated and revised Elizabeth Weinbloom April 30, 2011. Copyright held by GradeSaver.

William Schofield. "A journey to shock and enlighten." 2004-01-29. 2010-08-07. <http://www.guardian.co.uk/books/2004/jan/29/whitbreadbookawards2003.costabookaward>.

Charlotte Moore. "Just the facts, ma'am." 2003-05-24. 2010-06-08. <http://www.guardian.co.uk/books/2003/may/24/booksforchildrenandteenagers.bookerprize200

Haddon, Mark. "About." 2011-04-28. <http://www.tehomet.net/mark.php>.

Essay: Nothing Without Math

by Anonymous
September 29, 2009

Nothing Without Math

The novel The Curious Incident of the Dog in the Night-Time, by Mark Haddon, tells the story of part of Christopher Boone's life. Christopher Boone is a fifteen-year-old boy who has been diagnosed with high functioning Asperger's disease. He is also the narrator of the novel. Throughout the novel, Christopher tries to relate as many things as possible to math, because it makes him feel comfortable. Being a person who doesn't like change, Christopher likes math for it's consistency and predictability. Without this element of math, Christopher would not be the same character, and thus the novel would be a completely different book.

The reader notices right away that the chapters are not numbered as they would be in any other book. The first chapter starts out as chapter 2, and then the next chapter is 3, and the next is 5. Christopher Boone knows every prime number up to 7,057 (Haddon 2). Thus, he assigns the chapters of his book to consecutive prime numbers, just because this is something that he likes. Christopher tells us that "[he] think[s] prime number are like life. They are very logical but you could never work out the rules, even if you spent all your time thinking about them" (Haddon 12). Although this is not something that would change the storyline of the novel, if Christopher had no interest in math, the chapters would be numbered regularly instead, which in turn would take away from some of Christopher's character as being "strange" or "different".

Having Asperger's makes Christopher act "abnormal" in some ways. For example, he does not like to be touched. We see this displayed quite well when in the novel, Christopher actually hits a police man for touching him (Haddon 8). Christopher explains was he says that "[He] see[s] everything. That is why [he] doesn't like new places" (Haddon 140). There are also several other things that Christopher can not stand, and that make him feel extremely uneasy and frustrated. When Christopher finds himself in one of these predicaments, where he becomes too overwhelmed with the situation, he turns to math to calm him down. Christopher finds comfort in being able to complete math problems or puzzles, mainly because it gives him something to focus on other than all the things that may be going on around him. Christopher explains, "And then I tried to think about what I had to do, but I couldn't think because there were too many other things in my head, so I did a maths problem to make my head clearer" (Haddon 146). Math is one of the only things that he can do to contain himself. Therefore, if Christopher didn't like math, this would have been a completely different storyline because he could not have done or handled some of the things that he did.

One of the things that Christopher was face to handle in the novel was the different relationships with his mother and father. Christopher's mother and father are divorced, and live in two different places. The reader learns throughout the book more about Christopher's relationship with his parents, and the way they each approach his passion for math. Christopher's dad is a character that doesn't necessarily seem like he enjoys having to deal with him, and many could even argue that he is not equipped to handle him; however, when Christopher decides that he wants to take the A-level maths, his father is determined to get him in it. Christopher tells us that his father wasn't going to take no for an answer from the principle (Haddon 45). On the other hand, Christopher's mother does not understand that math is so important to Christopher. She responds "I don't know whether it's going to be possible" and "Let's talk about this some other time" when Christopher tells her about how he has to take his A level math exam (Haddon 202). Through this window of his desire for math, we can get a good idea about how much each of Christopher's parents actually care about and understand him. Without this, it would be very hard to ever tell that Christopher's dad actually does understand him, and that his mother does not.

When Christopher tells the reader about some of the problems or math activities that he does in his head when he needs to calm down, the reader gets a great insight to how intelligent Christopher is in math. Specifically what comes to mind is when Christopher is talking about The Monty Hall Problem. He even hints at saying math and more standard things are better than deep thought by saying "this shows that intuition can sometimes get things wrong" (Haddon 65). Also, Christopher has included an appendix in the back where he shows the proofs of some of the math that he was talking about in the novel (Haddon 223). When he is talking about these things, Christopher doesn't ever say that he finds these things difficult, and many readers probably gain most of the respect that they have for Christopher through this line of intelligence. If Christopher was not smart in math like he is, the reader would have a much different view of him, and many readers would find him much less fascinating. Along with this, Christopher's only hope of really succeeding and achieving something big is through this intelligence in math that he has. Christopher wants to go on and take more A level courses in Physics and other maths, and become a scientist. Aside from the fact that he would have to have special accommodations, this is a very achievable goal for Christopher. Most other subject areas require creative thinking, and are open ended, which Christopher simply can not handle. This is because Christopher only like things that are patterned and orderly, and where there is a clear answer. If he did not like math, there would probably be no hope of him going to college and getting a career.

The novel ends somewhat open ended, and all the reader knows is that Christopher does want to go on and pursue more math and try and gain a career.

"I am going to take further A level maths next year and pass it and get an A grade. And in two years' time I am going to take A level physics and get an A grade. And then when I've done that, I am going to go to university in another town. And then I will get a First Class Honors degree and I will become a scientist" (Haddon 220-21).

If we did not know this, meaning if Christopher had no desire for math, the book would have an even more unresolved feeling. Though it would not be a valid claim to say that this novel's theme is math, it is clearly a very important component to the story, and it would not be nearly the same without it. Math is one of the central ideas upon which the novel is written, and though it could be written excluding it, it would cause the story to lose so much of its richness and detail.

Works Cited

Haddon, Mark. The Curious Incident of the Dog in the Night-Time. New York: Vintage Books, 2003.

Quiz 1

1. **What is the first piece of information we are given in the novel?**
   A. The weather: it is cloudy and grey
   B. The time: 7 minutes after midnight
   C. That Mrs Shears' dog was dead
   D. That Christopher sees a dog on the ground

2. **What is the name of the dog that Christopher finds dead?**
   A. Muzzle
   B. Paddington
   C. Wellington
   D. Rufus

3. **What type of dog was Mrs Shear's dog?**
   A. A poodle
   B. A king charles spaniel
   C. A dalmatian
   D. An alsatian

4. **What is Christopher's full name?**
   A. Christopher John
   B. Christopher John Francis Boone
   C. Christopher Boone
   D. Christopher John Francis

5. **Who draws pictures of faces for Christopher so that he can understand different emotions?**
   A. Siobhan
   B. Mrs Shears
   C. His father
   D. His mother

6. **How does Christopher know Siobhan?**
   A. She is his aunt
   B. She is a teacher at his school
   C. She is a friend of his mother's
   D. She is his cousin

7. **Why does Christopher like dogs?**
    A. Because you always know what they are thinking, because they are faithful, do not lie and cannot talk
    B. Because they are playful and always like attention
    C. Because they like being cuddled
    D. Because dogs like to go out walking for long periods of time

8. **What is Christopher doing when Mrs Shears finds her dead dog for the first time?**
    A. Standing near the dog
    B. Crying next to the dog
    C. Kicking the dog
    D. Hugging the dog

9. **What kind of novel does Christopher say this is?**
    A. An animal novel
    B. A romance
    C. A murder mystery novel
    D. A sci-fi novel

10. **Who interrogates Christopher after Mrs Shears discovers what's happened to her dog?**
    A. Mr Shears
    B. The police
    C. His father
    D. A passer-by

11. **How old is Christopher?**
    A. 9
    B. 11
    C. 15
    D. 18

12. **When does Christopher start 'groaning'?**
    A. When there is too much information in his head from the outside world
    B. When he has to sit at the dinner table
    C. When he feels sad
    D. When he sees an animal in distress

13. **What does Christopher do when the policeman touches him?**
    A. He cries
    B. He cowers
    C. He hits him
    D. He stands up

14. **Why is Christopher arrested?**
    A. For lying
    B. For murder
    C. For manslaughter
    D. For assault

15. **How does Christopher number his chapters?**
    A. With cardinal number
    B. With pictures
    C. With prime number
    D. With letters

16. **According to Christopher, what happens in American if you find a prime number of over 100 digits longs?**
    A. You are arrested
    B. The government hides you away
    C. The CIA asks you to work for them
    D. The CIA buys it for $10 000

17. **Why does Christopher always wear a watch?**
    A. Because it feels nice
    B. Because he needs to know exactly what the time is
    C. Because it's fashionable
    D. Because it was a present from his father

18. **Who does Christopher tell the policeman makes up his family?**
    A. His uncle
    B. His father, uncle and grandmother (his mother is dead)
    C. His mother, uncle and grandmother (his father is dead)
    D. His grandmother and uncle

19. What does Christopher do instead of hugging?

    A. Stands back to back with the other person

    B. Winking

    C. Kissing

    D. Spreads the fingers on his left hand intoa fan so that his fingers and thumb touch the other persons'

20. What happens at the police station?

    A. Christopher is told off

    B. Christopher is given a caution

    C. Christopher is given biscuits

    D. Christopher is sentenced

21. Why doesn't Christopher ever tells lies?

    A. Because he can't

    B. Because he doesn't want to get into trouble

    C. Because he thinks God will punish him if he does

    D. Because he is a good person

22. What does Christopher's father tell him to do?

    A. To write a book

    B. Bury Wellington

    C. Keep his nose out of other people's business

    D. Try and find out who killed Wellington

23. How many years ago does Christopher think his mother died?

    A. Twenty

    B. Ten

    C. Two

    D. Five

24. What does 4 red cars in a row mean to Christopher?

    A. A Quite Good Day

    B. A Super Good Day

    C. A Good Day

    D. A Black Day

25. **What does 4 yellow cars in a row mean to Christopher?**
    A. A Quite Good Day
    B. A Super Good Day
    C. A Good Day
    D. A Black Day

Quiz 1 Answer Key

1. **(B)** The time: 7 minutes after midnight
2. **(C)** Wellington
3. **(A)** A poodle
4. **(B)** Christopher John Francis Boone
5. **(A)** Siobhan
6. **(B)** She is a teacher at his school
7. **(A)** Because you always know what they are thinking, because they are faithful, do not lie and cannot talk
8. **(D)** Hugging the dog
9. **(C)** A murder mystery novel
10. **(B)** The police
11. **(C)** 15
12. **(A)** When there is too much information in his head from the outside world
13. **(C)** He hits him
14. **(D)** For assault
15. **(C)** With prime number
16. **(D)** The CIA buys it for $10 000
17. **(B)** Because he needs to know exactly what the time is
18. **(B)** His father, uncle and grandmother (his mother is dead)
19. **(D)** Spreads the fingers on his left hand intoa fan so that his fingers and thumb touch the other persons'
20. **(B)** Christopher is given a caution
21. **(A)** Because he can't
22. **(C)** Keep his nose out of other people's business
23. **(C)** Two
24. **(C)** A Good Day
25. **(D)** A Black Day

Quiz 2

1. **What is Christopher's ideal job?**
   A. Sumo wrestler
   B. Astronaut
   C. Violinist
   D. Firefighter

2. **Why does Christopher start writing his story?**
   A. As an assignment for school
   B. Because his father told him to
   C. Because he has always wanted to be a novelist
   D. As a police report

3. **What did the get well card that Christopher made for his mother have on the front of it?**
   A. Red Cars
   B. Red Dogs
   C. Red Spaceships
   D. Yellow Cats

4. **What does Christopher think his mother died from?**
   A. Asthma
   B. A heart attack
   C. Falling from a ladder
   D. A dog bite

5. **Who comes over to look after Christopher and his father after Christopher's mother dies?**
   A. Rhodri
   B. Mrs Alexander
   C. Siobhan
   D. Mrs Shears

6. **What is Christopher's immediate reaction to the news that his mother is dead?**
   A. He is angry and runs around the house banging the walls
   B. Suspicious because she was only 38 which is young for someone to have a heartattack
   C. He feels guilty
   D. He starts crying

7. **Why doesn't Christopher always do what he is told?**
    A. Because he doesn't like being told what to do
    B. Because he is scared of doing what people say
    C. Because he says what people tell you is usually confusing and doesn't make sense
    D. Because he wants to wind people up

8. **Which person gives Christopher precise instructions so that the instructions make sense to him?**
    A. Siobhan
    B. His father
    C. His mother
    D. Wellington

9. **When Christopher starts his investigation, where does he go first?**
    A. School
    B. His mother's in London
    C. Mrs Shears' house
    D. His grandmother's

10. **When Reverend Peters comes to Christopher's school and Christopher asks him where heaven is, what does he say?**
    A. In space
    B. He says it's not in our universe
    C. Yorkshire
    D. In the ocean

11. **Why does Christopher think people believe in heaven?**
    A. Because they don't think logically
    B. Because they have been forced to by society
    C. Because they like the idea of a world outside our own
    D. Because they don't like the idea of dying

12. **Did Christopher see his mother's burial?**
    A. No, he was on a school trip at the time
    B. Even though she was buried, Christopher didn't see because he didn't go to the funeral
    C. Yes
    D. No, he wasn't at the funeral, and she was cremated

13. **What happened when Christopher punched Sarah at school?**
    A. Sarah punched him back
    B. He was put in detention
    C. The teacher hit him
    D. She fell unconscious and was rushed to A&E

14. **How does Christopher deal with people he doesn't know?**
    A. He is as sociable as possib;e
    B. He watches them until he knows that they are safe
    C. He asks them questions
    D. He just avoids them

15. **During his detective work, who offers Christopher tea and cake?**
    A. Mrs Alexander
    B. Mrs Shears
    C. His father
    D. Wellington

16. **What does Christopher think of the children at his school?**
    A. That they are stupid
    B. That they challenge him
    C. He really likes them
    D. That they are clever

17. **How does Christopher plan to prove he's not stupid?**
    A. By running a marathon
    B. By doing his Maths A-level
    C. By dropping out of school and starting a shop
    D. By doing his English A-level

18. **Who is the headmistress at Chistopher's school?**
    A. Siobhan
    B. Reverend Peters
    C. Mrs Strong
    D. Mrs Gascoyne

19. **What town does Christopher live in?**
    A. London
    B. Sydney
    C. Swindon
    D. York

20. **What does Christopher plan to do after A-levels?**
    A. Become a dance teacher
    B. A level Further Maths & Physics
    C. Buy a house
    D. Become an astonaut

21. **What is Christopher particular about when he eats his meals?**
    A. That he mixes all his food together
    B. That he says grace before every meal
    C. He makes sure each different food item is separate from any other
    D. He has to have ketchup with everything

22. **Why does Christopher think he'd be a good astonaut?**
    A. Because he has read up on being an astonaut
    B. Because he is strong, healthy and interested in the stars
    C. Being his father said he would be
    D. Because he is intelligent, understands how machines work and likes being along in tiny spaces

23. **When Christopher's father tells him to stop 'detecting', what implication does that have on the novel?**
    A. Christopher has to stop writing and so the novel must finish
    B. The novel becomes more boring
    C. Christopher has to read his father what he's written so far
    D. He can publish the novel as it is finished

24. **Why does Christopher not abandon the novel?**
    A. Because he has become addicted to writing
    B. Because 5 days later he sees 5 red cars in a row - making it a Super Good Day - so he knows something special will happen
    C. Because 5 days later he sees 5 orange cars in a row - making it a Super Good Day - so he knows something special will happen
    D. Because he hates his father

25. **Even though he has been told not to talk to the neighbours about Wellington, why does Christopher talk to Mrs Alexander?**
    A. Because he hates his father and refuses to do what he's told
    B. Because he misses his mother and wants a female figure in his life
    C. Because he wants to tell Mrs Alexander why he can't talk to her
    D. Because he has seen five red cars in a row and he thinks that talking to Mrs Alexander about Wellington may be the 'Super Good' thing that is going to happen

Quiz 2 Answer Key

1. **(B)** Astronaut
2. **(A)** As an assignment for school
3. **(A)** Red Cars
4. **(B)** A heart attack
5. **(D)** Mrs Shears
6. **(B)** Suspicious because she was only 38 which is young for someone to have a heartattack
7. **(C)** Because he says what people tell you is usually confusing and doesn't make sense
8. **(A)** Siobhan
9. **(C)** Mrs Shears' house
10. **(B)** He says it's not in our universe
11. **(D)** Because they don't like the idea of dying
12. **(D)** No, he wasn't at the funeral, and she was cremated
13. **(D)** She fell unconscious and was rushed to A&E
14. **(B)** He watches them until he knows that they are safe
15. **(A)** Mrs Alexander
16. **(A)** That they are stupid
17. **(B)** By doing his Maths A-level
18. **(D)** Mrs Gascoyne
19. **(C)** Swindon
20. **(B)** A level Further Maths & Physics
21. **(C)** He makes sure each different food item is separate from any other
22. **(D)** Because he is intelligent, understands how machines work and likes being along in tiny spaces
23. **(A)** Christopher has to stop writing and so the novel must finish
24. **(B)** Because 5 days later he sees 5 red cars in a row - making it a Super Good Day - so he knows something special will happen
25. **(D)** Because he has seen five red cars in a row and he thinks that talking to Mrs Alexander about Wellington may be the 'Super Good' thing that is going to happen

Quiz 3

1. **What vital information does Mrs Alexander impart to him?**
    - A. That she killed Wellington
    - B. That she is his grandmother
    - C. That his mother had an affair with Mr Shears
    - D. That Ed Boon is not really Christopher's father

2. **There is a column written by a woman with the highest IQ in the world - what is the name of her column?**
    - A. Dear Abby
    - B. Ask Marilyn
    - C. Ask Dorothy
    - D. Easy Answers

3. **Which does Christopher think is more reliable? Logic or Intuition?**
    - A. Neither
    - B. Intuition
    - C. Both
    - D. Logic

4. **Why does Christopher make a point of trying to include description in his novel?**
    - A. Because his father told him it was important to include description
    - B. In memory of his mother, who loved descriptive passages
    - C. Because Siobhan said that it was important to include description
    - D. Because he wants people to feel emotionally connected to his novel

5. **What is Christopher's favourite book?**
    - A. Hamlet
    - B. A Spot of Bother
    - C. Hound of the Baskervilles
    - D. Pride and Prejudice

6. **What does Christopher compare his memory to?**
    - A. An elephant's memory
    - B. An astronaut's
    - C. A DVD player
    - D. A VHS player

7. **What is Christopher watching when his father storms in and confronts him about his book?**
    A. Hamlet
    B. Winnie the Pooh
    C. Desperate Housewives
    D. Blue Planet

8. **Why doesn't Christopher immediately realize that his father is angry about having found his book?**
    A. Because he is thinking about what he's going to have for dinner
    B. Because he is laughing
    C. Because he is quiet to start with and not shouting
    D. Because he isn't concentrating

9. **When Christopher's father grabs him because he is angry about the book, what does Christopher do?**
    A. Starts to cry
    B. Tells him to stop touching him
    C. Hits him back
    D. Wets himself

10. **What does Christopher's father do with the book?**
    A. Puts it in the bin
    B. Puts in in the sink
    C. Throws it at Christopher
    D. Rips it into little pieces

11. **What colours does Christopher hate?**
    A. Blue and black
    B. Green and purple
    C. Yellow and brown
    D. Red and pink

12. **How does Ed plan to make it up to Christopher for hitting him?**
    A. Giving him a hug
    B. Taking him to the cinema
    C. Buying him a red car
    D. Taking him to Twycross Zoo

13. **When was the mystery of the Cottingley Fairies solved?**
    A. 1900
    B. 1917
    C. 1981
    D. 2001

14. **Where does Ed hide Christopher's bookin the end?**
    A. Under the sofa
    B. In a shoe
    C. In his shirt box
    D. In the bin

15. **When is Christopher allowed to look around his father's room?**
    A. At the weekend
    B. Anytime
    C. On Mondays
    D. Never

16. **What else does Christopher notice in his father's room?**
    A. A photo of his mother
    B. A letter addressed to Christopher
    C. Wellington's dog collar
    D. A teddy bear

17. **What does Christopher do when he hears his father coming back home?**
    A. Steals the letter out of his father's room
    B. Goes downstairs to meet him
    C. Pretends to be asleep
    D. Quickly tidies up

18. **Who does Christopher discover the letter is written by?**
    A. Mr Shears
    B. His father
    C. His mother
    D. Wellington

19. When was the letter from his mother written?

    A. A year and a half after she died

    B. A year and a half before she died

    C. Three days before

    D. Just before she died

20. How does Christopher think all mysteries will be solved?

    A. With faith

    B. By God

    C. By school teachers

    D. With science

21. How many letters does Christopher find from his mother?

    A. 4

    B. 12

    C. 43

    D. 106

22. After reading a few letter, what does Christopher realize?

    A. That his father has been lying to him and his mother is not dead

    B. That he is a very quick reader

    C. That his novel is going to be really exciting

    D. That his mother loves him

23. How does Christopher react to the revelation?

    A. He cries

    B. He rings all his friends to tell them

    C. He starts writing a new novel

    D. He is sick and passes out

24. What explanation does Ed give his son as to why he lied to him?

    A. To protect him

    B. To annoy Christopher's mother

    C. Because he was sad

    D. So that Christopher would live with him

25. **What information does Ed then tell his son?**
     A. That Christopher has brothers and sister
     B. That Christopher can take his A-Level in Maths
     C. That he is terminally ill
     D. That he killed Wellington

Quiz 3 Answer Key

1. **(C)** That his mother had an affair with Mr Shears
2. **(B)** Ask Marilyn
3. **(D)** Logic
4. **(C)** Because Siobhan said that it was important to include description
5. **(C)** Hound of the Baskervilles
6. **(C)** A DVD player
7. **(D)** Blue Planet
8. **(C)** Because he is quiet to start with and not shouting
9. **(C)** Hits him back
10. **(A)** Puts it in the bin
11. **(C)** Yellow and brown
12. **(D)** Taking him to Twycross Zoo
13. **(C)** 1981
14. **(C)** In his shirt box
15. **(D)** Never
16. **(B)** A letter addressed to Christopher
17. **(A)** Steals the letter out of his father's room
18. **(C)** His mother
19. **(A)** A year and a half after she died
20. **(D)** With science
21. **(C)** 43
22. **(A)** That his father has been lying to him and his mother is not dead
23. **(D)** He is sick and passes out
24. **(A)** To protect him
25. **(D)** That he killed Wellington

Quiz 4

1. **What does Christopher do after he hears the news?**
   A. Waits for his father to go to sleep and then between the wall of the shed and the fence
   B. Hugs his father
   C. Telephones his mother
   D. Writes a new chapter in his novel

2. **In the morning, when his father notices he's missing and then goes to look for him, what does Christopher do?**
   A. He locks himself in the house
   B. He decides to set out to find his mother
   C. He calls the police
   D. He goes to see Mrs Alexander

3. **Why does he decide to leave home?**
   A. To punish his father
   B. Because he is angry with his father
   C. Because he misses his mother
   D. Because he is scared of his father

4. **Christopher tells one of his neighbours everything that has happened. Which one?**
   A. Mrs Alexander
   B. Mr Apple
   C. Mr Shears
   D. Simon

5. **Who does he take with him on his journey to London?**
   A. Siobhan
   B. His baby sister
   C. His father
   D. His rat Toby

6. **Why doesn't Christopher like new places?**
   A. Because he finds new places tiring
   B. Because he gets scared of the people who might live there
   C. Because he notices everything and so it's always a lot for him to take in
   D. Because he gets home-sick

7. How does Christopher calm himself down?

    A. By thinking about his novel

    B. By focusing on math problems

    C. By thinking of his father

    D. By closing his eyes

8. When he's at the train station, who comes up to Christopher?

    A. A tramp

    B. Siobhan

    C. His mother

    D. A policeman

9. How does Christopher feel with the policeman there?

    A. Depressed

    B. Safer

    C. Happy

    D. Scared

10. What does the policeman help Christopher with?

    A. Speaking French

    B. Getting money out and buying a ticket

    C. Tying his shoelace

    D. Phoning his mother

11. Why does Christopher like timetables?

    A. Because he draws them in creative ways

    B. Because his mother encouraged him to make them

    C. Because it helps him to focus on his work

    D. Because 'they make sure you don't get lost in time'

12. What happens when Christopher gets on the train?

    A. He goes to sleep

    B. He starts to cry

    C. He calls his mother

    D. The policeman asks him to get off so that he can be reunited with his father

13. **What does the policeman do when he sees Christopher on the train?**
    A. Tells Christopher's father
    B. Tells Christopher's mother
    C. Decides to escort him to London
    D. Tries to get him off but doesn't manage to before the train starts
    moving

14. **How does Christopher get away from the policeman?**
    A. He hides under the seat
    B. He runs as fast as he can
    C. He punches the policeman
    D. He hides in a cupboard on the train

15. **Once he is off the train, what tube station does Christopher want to get to?**
    A. Holborn
    B. Liverpool Street
    C. Hammersmith
    D. Willesden Junction

16. **Why does Christopher moan on the tube platform?**
    A. Because he misses his father
    B. Because he is home-sick
    C. Because of the screeching sound of the trains pulling in
    D. Because he has lost Toby

17. **How does Christopher rescue Toby when he realizes he has escaped onto the train tracks?**
    A. He follows Toby onto the tracks and grabs him just before the train
    arrives
    B. He scoops him up with his hat
    C. He puts cheese out for him and he returns to Christopher
    D. He gets a policeman to rescue him

18. **What happens when he gets to his mothers house?**
    A. He cries
    B. He calls the police to tell them about Wellington
    C. Christopher tells her he thought she was dead and that his father lied
    D. He wishes he was back at his dad's

19. **What does Christopher have to go back to Swindon to do?**
     A. See his cousin
     B. His math A-level
     C. Say sorry to his father
     D. Bury Wellington

20. **Why does Christopher's mother leave Mr Shears?**
     A. Because she falls back in love with Ed
     B. Because Christopher doesn't like him
     C. Because she is bored of him
     D. Because he is rude to Christopher

21. **How is Christopher able to take his A-level?**
     A. The school arranges for an invigilator to come in
     B. His mother begs the exam board
     C. His father sits the exam for him
     D. He does the exam in Scotland

22. **Who does Christopher now live with?**
     A. Mrs Alexander
     B. Siobhan
     C. His father
     D. His mother

23. **Whose house does Christopher go to after school**
     A. Siobhan's
     B. Mrs Shears'
     C. His father's - until his mother picks him up after work
     D. His mother's - until his father picks him up after work

24. **How does Christopher's father try and make it up to him?**
     A. By buying him a new computer
     B. By writing him a letter
     C. By suggesting that they work on a project together where he proves to Christopher that he can be trusted
     D. By giving him a hug

25. **What does Christopher's father buy him?**
    A. A puppy
    B. A computer
    C. A rat
    D. An astronaut suit

Quiz 4 Answer Key

1. **(A)** Waits for his father to go to sleep and then between the wall of the shed and the fence
2. **(B)** He decides to set out to find his mother
3. **(D)** Because he is scared of his father
4. **(A)** Mrs Alexander
5. **(D)** His rat Toby
6. **(C)** Because he notices everything and so it's always a lot for him to take in
7. **(B)** By focusing on math problems
8. **(D)** A policeman
9. **(B)** Safer
10. **(B)** Getting money out and buying a ticket
11. **(D)** Because 'they make sure you don't get lost in time'
12. **(D)** The policeman asks him to get off so that he can be reunited with his father
13. **(D)** Tries to get him off but doesn't manage to before the train starts moving
14. **(D)** He hides in a cupboard on the train
15. **(D)** Willesden Junction
16. **(C)** Because of the screeching sound of the trains pulling in
17. **(A)** He follows Toby onto the tracks and grabs him just before the train arrives
18. **(C)** Christopher tells her he thought she was dead and that his father lied
19. **(B)** His math A-level
20. **(D)** Because he is rude to Christopher
21. **(A)** The school arranges for an invigilator to come in
22. **(D)** His mother
23. **(C)** His father's - until his mother picks him up after work
24. **(C)** By suggesting that they work on a project together where he proves to Christopher that he can be trusted
25. **(A)** A puppy

Quiz 5

1. **What does Christopher plan to do in the future?**
   A. His further math, physics A-level and then a degree and then become a scientist
   B. Join the circus
   C. Start a charity
   D. Move back in with his dad

Quiz 5 Answer Key

1. (**A**) His further math, physics A-level and then a degree and then become a scientist

ClassicNotes

GrAdeSaver™

Getting you the grade since 1999™

Other ClassicNotes from GradeSaver™

1984
Absalom, Absalom
Adam Bede
The Adventures of Augie
    March
The Adventures of
    Huckleberry Finn
The Adventures of Tom
    Sawyer
The Aeneid
Agamemnon
The Age of Innocence
The Alchemist (Coelho)
The Alchemist (Jonson)
Alice in Wonderland
All My Sons
All Quiet on the Western
    Front
All the King's Men
All the Pretty Horses
Allen Ginsberg's Poetry
The Ambassadors
American Beauty
And Then There Were
    None
Angela's Ashes
Animal Farm
Anna Karenina
Anthem
Antigone
Antony and Cleopatra
Aristotle's Ethics
Aristotle's Poetics
Aristotle's Politics
As I Lay Dying
As You Like It

Astrophil and Stella
Atlas Shrugged
Atonement
The Awakening
Babbitt
The Bacchae
Bartleby the Scrivener
The Bean Trees
The Bell Jar
Beloved
Benito Cereno
Beowulf
Bhagavad-Gita
Billy Budd
Black Boy
Bleak House
Bless Me, Ultima
Blindness
The Bloody Chamber
Bluest Eye
The Bonfire of the
    Vanities
The Book of the Duchess
    and Other Poems
The Book Thief
Brave New World
Breakfast at Tiffany's
Breakfast of Champions
The Brief Wondrous Life
    of Oscar Wao
The Brothers Karamazov
The Burning Plain and
    Other Stories
A Burnt-Out Case
By Night in Chile
Call of the Wild

Candide
The Canterbury Tales
Cat on a Hot Tin Roof
Cat's Cradle
Catch-22
The Catcher in the Rye
The Caucasian Chalk
    Circle
Charlotte's Web
The Cherry Orchard
The Chocolate War
The Chosen
A Christmas Carol
Christopher Marlowe's
    Poems
Chronicle of a Death
    Foretold
Civil Disobedience
Civilization and Its
    Discontents
A Clockwork Orange
The Color of Water
The Color Purple
Comedy of Errors
Communist Manifesto
A Confederacy of
    Dunces
Confessions
Connecticut Yankee in
    King Arthur's Court
The Consolation of
    Philosophy
Coriolanus
The Count of Monte
    Cristo
The Country Wife

For our full list of over 250 Study Guides, Quizzes,
Sample College Application Essays, Literature Essays and E-texts, visit:

www.gradesaver.com

ClassicNotes

GrↄdeSaver™

Getting you the grade since 1999™

Other ClassicNotes from GradeSaver™

In Our Time
In the Time of the
 Butterflies
Inherit the Wind
An Inspector Calls
Into the Wild
Invisible Man
The Island of Dr. Moreau
Jane Eyre
Jazz
The Jew of Malta
Joseph Andrews
The Joy Luck Club
Julius Caesar
The Jungle
Jungle of Cities
Kama Sutra
Kate Chopin's Short
 Stories
Kidnapped
King Lear
The Kite Runner
Last of the Mohicans
Leaves of Grass
The Legend of Sleepy
 Hollow
Leviathan
Libation Bearers
Life is Beautiful
Life of Pi
Light In August
The Lion, the Witch and
 the Wardrobe
Little Women
Lolita

Long Day's Journey Into
 Night
Look Back in Anger
Lord Jim
Lord of the Flies
The Lord of the Rings:
 The Fellowship of the
 Ring
The Lord of the Rings:
 The Return of the
 King
The Lord of the Rings:
 The Two Towers
A Lost Lady
The Lottery and Other
 Stories
Love in the Time of
 Cholera
The Love Song of J.
 Alfred Prufrock
The Lovely Bones
Lucy
Macbeth
Madame Bovary
Maggie: A Girl of the
 Streets and Other
 Stories
Manhattan Transfer
Mankind: Medieval
 Morality Plays
Mansfield Park
The Marrow of Tradition
The Master and
 Margarita
MAUS

The Mayor of
 Casterbridge
Measure for Measure
Medea
Merchant of Venice
Metamorphoses
The Metamorphosis
Middlemarch
A Midsummer Night's
 Dream
Moby Dick
A Modest Proposal and
 Other Satires
Moll Flanders
Mother Courage and Her
 Children
Mrs. Dalloway
Much Ado About
 Nothing
My Antonia
Mythology
Native Son
Nickel and Dimed: On
 (Not) Getting By in
 America
Night
Nine Stories
No Exit
Northanger Abbey
Notes from Underground
O Pioneers
The Odyssey
Oedipus Rex or Oedipus
 the King
Of Mice and Men
The Old Man and the Sea

For our full list of over 250 Study Guides, Quizzes,
Sample College Application Essays, Literature Essays and E-texts, visit:

www.gradesaver.com

ClassicNotes

Gr*A*deSaver™

Getting you the grade since 1999™

Other ClassicNotes from GradeSaver™

Oliver Twist
On Liberty
On the Road
One Day in the Life of
    Ivan Denisovich
One Flew Over the
    Cuckoo's Nest
One Hundred Years of
    Solitude
Oroonoko
Othello
Our Town
The Outsiders
Pale Fire
Pamela: Or Virtue
    Rewarded
Paradise Lost
A Passage to India
The Pearl
Percy Shelley: Poems
Perfume: The Story of a
    Murderer
Persepolis: The Story of
    a Childhood
Persuasion
Phaedra
Phaedrus
The Piano Lesson
The Picture of Dorian
    Gray
Poe's Poetry
Poe's Short Stories
Poems of W.B. Yeats:
    The Rose
Poems of W.B. Yeats:
    The Tower

The Poems of William
    Blake
The Poetry of Robert
    Frost
The Poisonwood Bible
Pope's Poems and Prose
Portrait of the Artist as a
    Young Man
Pride and Prejudice
The Prince
The Professor's House
Prometheus Bound
Pudd'nhead Wilson
Pygmalion
Rabbit, Run
A Raisin in the Sun
The Real Life of
    Sebastian Knight
Rebecca
The Red Badge of
    Courage
The Remains of the Day
The Republic
Rhinoceros
Richard II
Richard III
The Rime of the Ancient
    Mariner
Rip Van Winkle and
    Other Stories
The Road
Robinson Crusoe
Roll of Thunder, Hear
    My Cry
Romeo and Juliet
A Room of One's Own

A Room With a View
A Rose For Emily and
    Other Short Stories
Rosencrantz and
    Guildenstern Are
    Dead
Salome
The Scarlet Letter
The Scarlet Pimpernel
The Seagull
The Secret Life of Bees
Secret Sharer
Sense and Sensibility
A Separate Peace
Shakespeare's Sonnets
Shantaram
Short Stories of Ernest
    Hemingway
Siddhartha
Silas Marner
Sir Gawain and the
    Green Knight
Sister Carrie
Six Characters in Search
    of an Author
Slaughterhouse Five
Snow Falling on Cedars
The Social Contract
Something Wicked This
    Way Comes
Song of Roland
Song of Solomon
Sons and Lovers
The Sorrows of Young
    Werther
The Sound and the Fury

For our full list of over 250 Study Guides, Quizzes,
Sample College Application Essays, Literature Essays and E-texts, visit:

www.gradesaver.com

ClassicNotes

GrAdeSaver™

Getting you the grade since 1999™

Other ClassicNotes from GradeSaver™

The Spanish Tragedy
Spenser's Amoretti and
  Epithalamion
Spring Awakening
The Stranger
A Streetcar Named
  Desire
Sula
The Sun Also Rises
Tale of Two Cities
The Taming of the Shrew
The Tempest
Tender is the Night
Tess of the D'Urbervilles
Their Eyes Were
  Watching God
Things Fall Apart
The Things They Carried
A Thousand Splendid
  Suns
The Threepenny Opera
Through the Looking
  Glass
Thus Spoke Zarathustra
The Time Machine
Titus Andronicus
To Build a Fire
To Kill a Mockingbird
To the Lighthouse
The Tortilla Curtain
Treasure Island
Trifles
Troilus and Cressida
Tropic of Cancer
Tropic of Capricorn
Tuesdays With Morrie

The Turn of the Screw
Twelfth Night
Twilight
Ulysses
Uncle Tom's Cabin
Utopia
Vanity Fair
A Very Old Man With
  Enormous Wings
Villette
The Visit
Volpone
Waiting for Godot
Waiting for Lefty
Walden
Washington Square
The Waste Land
Where the Red Fern
  Grows
White Fang
White Noise
White Teeth
Who's Afraid of Virginia
  Woolf
Wide Sargasso Sea
Winesburg, Ohio
The Winter's Tale
The Woman Warrior
Wordsworth's Poetical
  Works
Woyzeck
A Wrinkle in Time
Wuthering Heights
The Yellow Wallpaper
Yonnondio: From the
  Thirties

For our full list of over 250 Study Guides, Quizzes,
Sample College Application Essays, Literature Essays and E-texts, visit:

www.gradesaver.com

Made in the USA
Lexington, KY
07 August 2011